Dr. Kookie, You're Right!

Mike Royko

A PLUME BOOK

To Judy and Sam

PLUME

Published by the Penguin Group

Penguin Books USA Inc., 375 Hudson Street, New York, New York 10014, U.S.A.
Penguin Books Ltd, 27 Wrights Lane, London W8 5TZ, England
Penguin Books Australia Ltd, Ringwood, Victoria, Australia
Penguin Books Canada Ltd, 2801 John Street,
Markham, Ontario, Canada L3R 1B4
Penguin Books (N.Z.) Ltd, 182–190 Wairau Road, Auckland 10, New Zealand

Penguin Books Ltd, Registered Offices: Harmondsworth, Middlesex, England

Published by Plume, an imprint of New American Library, a division of
Penguin Books USA Inc. Previously published in a Dutton edition.

First Plume Printing, November, 1990
10 9 8 7 6 5 4 3 2 1

REGISTERED TRADEMARK—MARCA REGISTRADA

Library of Congress Cataloging-in-Publication Data

Royko, Mike, 1933–
Dr. Kookie, you're right / Mike Royko.
p.   cm.
Reprint. Originally published: New York : Dutton, 1989.
ISBN 0-452-26515-0
1. Chicago (Ill.)—Social life and customs—Humor.   2. United
States—Social life and customs—1971–   —Humor.   I. Title.
F548.52.R65   1990
977.3'11— dc20   90–39979
                                                       CIP

Printed in the United States of America
Original hardcover design by REM Studio.

Contents

HALLELUJAH!

PADDED CELL 1
"GIMME, GIMME!"

PADDED CELL 2
"LIFESTYLES OF THE WHO?"

PADDED CELL 3
"DOUBLE-LOCK THE DOORS!"

PADDED CELL 4
"CAN'T WE STILL BE FRIENDS?"

PADDED CELL 5
"CAN'T WE PLAY FOR FUN?"

Hallelujah!

These Heretics Pay
Through the Nose

February 17, 1989

Our government and many others have denounced the Ayatollah Khomeini for the death sentence he placed upon the author of a novel that has offended the Islamic world. And for offering a bounty of up to $3 million for anyone who bumps off the writer.

Individuals throughout the world are expressing horror that a "hit" should be ordered for someone merely for writing a work of fiction.

As Studs Terkel, the famous Chicago author and radio interviewer, told me: "I was going to have Salman Rushdie on my show to talk about his book. And now he's got to hide in England 'cuz they're going to kill him. Has the world gone nuts?"

But I can't share this indignation. Death, after all, is the punishment for blasphemy in the Moslem religion.

And I can sympathize with the true believers of that religion whose sensibilities have been offended.

That's because I belong to a religion that also carries a severe punishment for those who would dare scoff at our beliefs.

As I've written before, I am a member of the Church of Asylumism and believe it is the one and only true faith.

For those who are not familiar with the Church of Asylumism, I will provide a brief history. Then I'll explain how we punish heretics.

Our church was founded by Dr. I. M. Kookie, one of the world's leading experts on lots of things. In our church, he is called the Prophet Kookie.

As Prophet Kookie has revealed in the Book of Kook, man is not native to this planet. He did not evolve from monkeys, as some people believe, or descend from Adam and Eve, as others insist.

Millions of years ago, a highly advanced race of peaceful, happy beings on a distant planet had a perfect society. But they developed a social problem. A few hundred of them became deranged. Their madness took different forms. Some stole or became violent. Others tried to become lawyers. Some wanted to form political parties. And a few claimed that God spoke to them and told them how everybody should live.

So they were rounded up, put on a spaceship, and a search was made for an uninhabited planet that would serve as an asylum. They found this planet.

As the Book of Kook reveals: "The spaceship crew that dumped them here named the planet Earth, because in their language, the word Earth means 'booby hatch.'"

Thus, we are all descended from this group of transplanted lunatics, which explains man's eccentric behavior throughout recorded history.

Many people don't share our beliefs. And that's fine. We don't impose our faith on others. In fact, we try to limit the membership of the Church of Asylumism. As Prophet Kookie wrote in the Book of Kook:

"It would be unwise to convert masses to our faith. There are not enough shrinks to go around."

However, we do expect to be accorded the same respect that we extend to those of other faiths.

If others wish to fight holy wars, blow each other up, whip, flog, discriminate, ostracize, highjack, riot and murder—all in the name of religion—we do not criticize or deny them their means of showing devotion to their faith.

To the contrary. As the Book of Kook tells us:

"It just shows that we're right. This is one big booby hatch."

However, we expect the same respect to be shown to our faith. And we have ways of punishing those who fail to show proper respect.

Unfortunately, this has occurred in recent days.

After I revealed the existence of the Church of Asylumism, I received numerous calls and letters from those who were, to say the least, rude.

One woman called and shrieked: "You and this guy Kookie sound like a couple of nuts."

A man phoned and said: "This is the most ridiculous religion I have ever heard of, and this Prophet Kookie ought to be in a nut house himself."

And a letter came from a person who said: "You and this Kookie person will fry in hell for spreading this kind of garbage."

Well, it is one thing to insult my faith. I hold only the title of High Inmate in the Church of the Asylumism. We do not have titles such as deacon, bishop, rabbi or ayatollah.

Our rankings are Inmate, High Inmate, Ward Attendant, Shrink, High Shrink and, of course, the Prophet. (Should we ever have our own religious TV show, his title will be changed to the Profit.)

There is no penalty for insulting the rest of us. But we do not tolerate any slurs against the Prophet Kookie. As the Book of Kook says on this subject:

"The Prophet Kookie is not to be insulted, abused, ridiculed or have his hubcaps stolen.

"The punishment for these offenses is severe. Anyone who violates this rule will be sentenced to having his or her nose tweaked."

So, with the greatest solemnity, I must announce that those who have insulted and ridiculed the Prophet Kookie now face retribution.

You have been sentenced to having your noses tweaked. And, as High Inmate, I am offering a one-dollar reward to those who tweak the nose of those who have committed the offense.

This bounty has been approved by the Prophet Kookie. In fact, he is so offended, he has said:

"If the offender has a cold and a runny nose, the bounty is $1.50."

You have been warned.

New Film on Jesus Causes Holy Mess

August 12, 1988

"What'ya think?" Slats Grobnik asked. "Should we go see it?"

See what?

● 6

"You know, that movie about Jesus that's got everybody foaming at the mouth."

Ah, you mean *The Last Temptation of Christ.*

"That's it. You wanna go?"

Well, it would be interesting to see what the flap is all about. Do you want to go?

"I dunno. I like happy endings, but from what I read, it sounds like a downer."

Well, it's hard to have a happy ending with a crucifixion.

"No, it can be done. I saw a Bible movie on the late show that finished okay. Victor Mature was a gladiator. He started out as a mean guy, but after the crucifixion he turned into a good guy, although he still looked like a mope, but that's the way Victor Mature always looked. I was falling asleep near the end, but I think he turned in his sword and armor for a burlap wardrobe and that made him holy. Hey, why is it that if you're going to be holy, you got to wear clothes that itch?"

I don't know, but that was your standard Hollywood Bible film. I gather that *The Last Temptation of Christ* is something quite different.

"Yeah, I don't remember any Catholic cardinals or Jerry Falwell or anybody getting mad about Victor Mature. Or any of those other old movies where there would be a lot of clouds and lightning jumping around the sky and then you hear God talking. Except it wasn't God, it was some guy with a deep radio announcer voice. Why didn't they get mad when some guy who did soap commercials played God?"

Because in *The Last Temptation of Christ*, Jesus is portrayed as someone with human frailties, subject to the same temptations as the rest of us.

"Like what? They didn't have racetracks in those days."

Well, there is a scene in which He has a dream that He gets married.

"He dreams about it? What's wrong with that? It's only if you actually get married when you're wide awake that you have troubles."

Yes, but in the movie He also dreams about having sex, and some of it is shown on the screen.

"Huh. At my age, I dream about having sex, too, but to be honest, I wouldn't want to see myself doing it on a movie screen."

The point is, Jesus is portrayed as having self-doubts, character flaws, not being sure of his own divinity.

"Sort of like a split personality?"

From what I've read, yes.

"I can see where that could be a problem. In those days, they didn't have shrinks. And even if they had one, he probably couldn't have afforded it on a carpenter's paycheck. Especially before they got union scale. So, are we going to go see it?"

I don't know. There will probably be pickets at the theater. People are really angry. Fundamentalists, Catholics, the whole range of Christianity is up in arms.

"That don't make sense. It's just a movie, some pictures on a screen with a soundtrack. If they don't like it, they should just stay home, read their Bible and not go to see it."

No, they believe it is blasphemous, an insult to Christ, morally unacceptable. And that it could undermine the faith of those who do see it.

"I don't understand that kind of thinking. If the movie is so terrible, then why didn't God hit the studio with a bolt of lightning? He used to do stuff like that, turning somebody into salt, flooding the whole world, getting a guy swallowed by a big fish. So if He let them make the movie, He can't be too upset about it, right? I mean, it wouldn't have even taken a lightning bolt to stop them. A stagehand strike would have done it."

Only the theologians can answer your questions, and I'm not sure about them, since they can't agree on the movie.

"Well, I don't get it. Why didn't all those people get mad when George Burns played God? I mean, if they don't like Jesus having weird dreams, what about God smoking a cigar and doing parlor tricks?"

George Burns playing God was meant to be funny.

"It was?"

Sure, that was the whole idea—God as a stand-up comic.

"Well, they fooled me. Considering the shape the world is in, I thought it was a documentary."

Say Yer Prayers, Ron, or Shut Up

August 31, 1984

While driving through Arkansas last week, I tuned into a nighttime radio call-in show just in time to hear a rustic ask the host of the show: "How come all them liberals are agin' God?"

The show's host blandly said: "I just don't understand that myself. Maybe somebody out there has the answer and will call us."

Nobody called to explain the evil ways of liberals. But more significantly, nobody called to dispute the wacky statement.

There's little doubt the Reverend Jerry Falwell and

the rest of the right wing, TV Bible-thumpers have done their job well. They've managed to convince a large segment of the population that God is a conservative Republican.

Among those who have seen the light are President Reagan, who is now saying that "religion and politics are necessarily related" and this relationship "has worked to the benefit of the nation."

And, echoing the Falwell crowd, he says that those who are against such things as school prayer are "intolerant of religion."

I'm not sure what Reagan means when he says that religion and politics are necessarily related.

I've spent much of my adult life listening to politicians telling lies with a straight face, double-dealing, double-talking, sidestepping and backtracking.

What religion prescribes that kind of behavior?

Take President Reagan. The way he talks about God and religion, you would think he spends half of his time on a special hot line to heaven.

Yet he hardly ever sets foot in a church. He says that going to church would cause extraordinary security problems. That may be so. But he manages to overcome security problems to make speeches before large groups of bankers and big business men. Are they less dangerous than church congregations?

Of course, there's nothing wrong with Reagan not going to church. He can, as his staff points out, seek spiritual guidance anywhere. He can pray in his living quarters, in the Oval Office, in his jet or helicopter or body-building room.

But how can we be sure he does? And, for that matter, how can we be sure that those on his staff do any praying?

I raise those questions because of Mr. Reagan's snippy remarks about organized school prayer and the alleged intolerance of those who oppose it.

Reagan and Falwell and others who are pushing school prayer have little patience with those who say that there's nothing to stop kids from praying silently in school any time they wish. They can pray in the classroom, the school yard, the gymnasium, the hallway, anywhere.

But that's not enough. I suspect that they don't trust kids to pray on their own. So they want a teacher to lead the prayers.

Here we have the President of the United States asking us to take his word that he prays. Yet he doesn't trust the schoolchildren of this nation to offer up a few silent words of their own. And that includes the many kids who go to church on Sunday, which Reagan doesn't do.

If Reagan is really sincere about the importance of daily prayer in the school, then why doesn't he set an example by establishing a firm policy of daily prayer in the White House? Better yet, on the White House lawn, where we could see him on TV.

The entire staff—from secretaries on up to the top man—could gather each morning to pray aloud for wisdom and goodness and all the usual virtues.

If you think about it, who is in greater need of wisdom and goodness—some runny-nosed eight-year-old or the powerful men of the White House who are shaping the destiny of the nation and planet?

And why limit it to the White House staff? It might also include all cabinet members and their staffs. They can surely use wisdom and goodness. Who can't? And what about the joint chiefs of staff? Do we have any idea if they pray? Or what they pray for?

Naturally, nobody would be required to do this. If some presidential aides or cabinet officers have personal reasons to decline, that would be their right. After all, the classroom prayer advocates say schoolchildren would have that right. Of course, if a White House big shot did decide to reject prayers, some people might say: "What's his problem? Doesn't he believe in God, hmmmmm?"

There might also be a problem finding a suitable, all-purpose prayer that wouldn't offend anyone—which is what they have in mind for the schools. That isn't easy, since there are so many religions in this country.

But these are problems that can be overcome. And, if he finds overcoming them difficult, the President can always pray for guidance.

Of course, if he does that privately, too, we can never be sure, can we?

TV Preachers Get
All the Compassion

February 23, 1988

"If I had it all to do over again," Slats Grobnik said, "I think I'd have become one of those TV preachers."

I've never thought of you as having deep religious convictions.

"Nah, that's not why," he said.

Ah, then it's the money that interests you. All those little old ladies sending in contributions.

"Yeah, that would be okay. I like a Rolex watch and a private jet as much as the next guy. But there's something even better than that."

Such as?

"Well, I was watching this guy Jimmy Swaggart on TV, with his lips trembling and his nose running, crying his eyes out and blubbering about how he had sinned because he was with a hooker in a motel."

● 12

Yes, a sad and humiliating display.

"Sad? What was so sad about it?"

Well, the poor man had to stand up before a nation-wide TV audience and confess that he had been guilty of a weakness of the flesh.

"Yes, but then did you see what happened next?"

No, my eyes were blurred with tears of compassion.

"Then I'll tell you what happened. His wife walks over and gives him a big hug."

Yes, I do remember seeing that.

"Well?"

Well, what?

"Who do we know that ever gets a hug from his wife when she finds out he's been messing around?"

Now that you mention it, I can't think of anyone.

"You bet you can't. If I did something like that, the only thing my wife would hug me with would be a piece of piano wire when I had my back turned."

But if you explained that you realize it was a sin and you repent, she might be understanding.

"Oh, sure. Guys do that all the time. A guy comes home and the wife yells: 'My friend Gladys saw you going in the Beddy Bye Motel with a hooker when you were supposed to be bowling.' And the husband says: 'Oh, Lordy, the devil made me do it. But I repent so let us pray together. Now, what's for dinner?' "

It's possible. The devil works considerable mischief.

"Sure. Then the wife says: 'Okay, you tell the judge the devil made you go to that motel. But my lawyer is going to tell the judge that I want the house, the furnishings, the car, the kids, your paycheck, and you can go get a room at the YMCA, you creep.' "

I suppose that Swaggart's wife is more understanding than most.

"Yeah, and so was Tammy. The way Tammy acted, you'd think that Jimmy hadn't done anything more than get caught peeking at a copy of *Penthouse.* Hey, you know what my wife told me after we got married?"

As I recall, she said you'd have to take more than one bath a week.

"Besides that. She said that because she loved me so much and I was such a great guy, if she ever found out that I was playing around, she'd wait until I was sleeping before she let me have it with an ice pick because she wouldn't want me to suffer."

She's always had a kindly manner.

"And remember what happened to lover boy Charlie with the skinny mustache when his wife found out about him and Pearl the waitress?"

Yeah, he had that unfortunate accident.

"Accident? Who ever heard of a woman accidentally spilling a pot of hot coffee on her husband at three o'clock in the morning when he's in bed sleeping? And remember where she spilled it? He walked like a duck for about a year."

But you must keep in mind that these TV clergymen and their followers believe in redemption through prayer.

"Yeah, I noticed that. Jimmy and Tammy say they are praying for Swaggart, even though he blew the whistle on Jimmy. He even said little Jimmy was some kind of wart."

I believe he said that Bakker was a cancer on the body of Christ.

"Right. So if little Jimmy was a cancer, what's that make Swaggart?"

In fairness to Swaggart, he says he did not actually have sex with the harlot. He simply sat there in his jogging suit watching her do something or other.

"Okay, we'll give him credit for that. Maybe he's not a cancer, but just some kind of a peeping eye."

Fair enough. But I still think it is touching that his wife would be that forgiving. As Swaggart said of her on TV:

"God never gave a man a better helpmate, a companion to stand beside him."

"Yeah, but if my wife ever catches me, I'm gonna pray that I have a wonderful helpmate, a companion to stand beside me."

And I'm sure your wife will do exactly that.

"Wife? I'm talking about a lawyer who knows the judge."

Justice Triumphs
Over Loudmouths

March 22, 1984

Every so often a jury returns a verdict that is so satisfyingly just, it makes you want to cheer. In the last week, we've had two of them.

One received national attention: the case of the tavern gang rape that ended in a guilty verdict and the rapists' friends and families rioting outside the courthouse.

They were indignant because the jury didn't believe one of the rapists, who said the victim eagerly agreed to have sex with him on a pool table in the tavern.

It's a standard part of most rape defenses that (a) it was the woman's idea and (b) the woman has a history of being wanton.

But this is the first time I ever heard a rapist say the victim seduced him on a tavern pool table. Even if his version were true, he should still go to jail on the grounds that he is a slob. In a nation with more than a million motels, there's no excuse for such behavior on a pool table.

15 ●

The other trial, which received less attention than it deserved, struck a blow against one of the greatest menaces to civilized life: the chronic, gossipy busybody.

They're found in every city neighborhood, small town, workplace and tavern: people who can't keep their noses out of the private lives of others.

In this case, the busybodies were the elders of the fundamentalist Church of Christ in the small town of Collinsville, Oklahoma.

One of the members of their congregation was an attractive young nurse, in her early thirties, divorced with four children.

Some of the elders began to suspect that the nurse was having an affair with a man who lived in the town. The nurse and her male friend weren't exactly wrestling around on tavern pool tables. But somebody spotted his car in her driveway, and that got tongues wagging.

So the elders finally spoke to the man, who admitted it, although he wasn't a member of the church. Just a spineless sort, I guess.

They confronted the woman and accused her of "fornication" and of not going to church often enough. And they told her that she would have to stand before the entire congregation and admit what she had done, repent her sin of fornication and ask them all to forgive her.

That struck the nurse as being far too stressful a way to spend a Sunday morning. So she refused. But she did promise not to see her boyfriend anymore.

Later, though, the man gave her and one of her kids a lift in his car. And who should be lurking in her driveway when she and the man got home? The church elders.

So they preached to her some more and told her that they were going to tell the entire congregation about her sinful conduct.

She begged and pleaded for them not to. Maybe movie stars don't mind talking about their sleeping habits to *People* magazine, but a small-town nurse doesn't need that kind of notoriety.

Nope, the elders said. The rules of the church required that they blab about her sex life to everyone.

So she offered what appeared to be a reasonable solution. She gave them a letter resigning from the church. If she was no longer a member, they wouldn't have to concern themselves with her sex life, her soul or who was praying in her driveway. Nope, they said. She couldn't quit. They had to kick her out.

So they went ahead and blabbed, even after she said she was leaving their church. They stood up in church and told the whole congregation, which amounted to about 5 percent of the entire population of the town, what a fornicator she was.

And they ordered that she be shunned by the congregation, although she wasn't eager for their companionship anyway.

Then they went home and ate Sunday dinner and felt righteous.

But the nurse went to see a lawyer and felt mad as hell.

The result was a lawsuit against the church and three elders, charging invasion of privacy. The trial was held recently and the jury got as mad as the nurse did. It awarded her $390,000 in damages, and some of the jurors said they wanted to give her more, but hadn't understood the judge's instructions.

Now it is possible that the nurse will wind up owning the church property. And if that doesn't cover the $390,000, she can probably go after some of the elders' property, such as their homes.

But the church elders are as unrepentant about their busybody activities as she was about her private life. One of them said they did it only because they loved her and were worried about her soul.

Well, the next time they worry about some woman's soul, they would be wise not to do their worrying in her driveway.

Such Christians
Prey on the Mind

June 9, 1986

An anti-abortion minister in California has publicly urged people to pray for the death of Supreme Court Justice William Brennan, whom he blames for millions of abortions. In taking this action, the minister may have started a national trend.

I recently ran into a couple who favor the right of individuals to have abortions and asked them how they felt about the minister's suggestion.

They said: "We are going to fight back with our prayers."

How?

"We're praying that the noses of that minister and others like him fall off so they won't be sticking them in other people's personal lives."

The loss of a nose is rather harsh, isn't it?

"Not really. There are other parts of the body we could pray fall off that would be even more embarrassing to him, and we might do that, too."

Later in the day, I mentioned this to a couple who are against abortions.

"Our noses, hmmmm?" they said angrily. "Well, we are going to get back at them. We are going to pray that they become bald."

But baldness isn't that unusual or serious.

"It is for women."

I thought it only fair that I should pass this threat along to the pro-abortion couple.

"Baldness?" They gasped. "All right, we're going to retaliate. We are going to pray that they have to undergo prolonged and expensive root canal work, but that their teeth fall out anyway."

I was starting to understand how it feels to be a war correspondent. And I relayed the threat of teeth loss to the anti-abortion couple.

"We anticipated something like that," they said, "so we're already praying."

For what?

"Waxy buildup in their ears."

Horrible.

"And uncomfortable, incurable, lifelong hiccups."

You really mean business.

"They're going to know the meaning of a terrible swift sword."

I conveyed the latest threat to the pro-abortion couple. They were visibly shaken as they said: "We knew that war was hell."

What are you going to do?

"We're going to press the button—the ultimate weapon."

I'm almost afraid to ask what it is. But tell me anyway.

"We are going to pray that the entire anti-abortion crowd will spend the rest of their lives plagued by uncontrollable and chronic flatulence."

You can't mean it.

"They'll be embarrassed to death."

But what about all the innocent bystanders?

"History tells us that the innocent are often victims in such conflicts. It can't be helped."

Wait. Reconsider. Negotiate.

"It's too late. Let us pray."

As this depressing day was ending, I joined my friend Slats Grobnik for a beer and told him about the exchange of hostile prayers.

"You sound worried," he said.

Of course I'm worried. If those prayers are fulfilled, it would wreak havoc on our society.

Slats thought for a long moment, then said: "You know about my boss, don't you?"

You've spoken of him often. How you should have his job. How much you loathe the cruel, evil man.

"That's right," Slats said. "But there's something I never told you."

What's that?

"For twenty-five years, I have gone to church on my way to work every morning and I've prayed for the same thing."

Don't tell me.

"Yeah, I've prayed that this guy croaks. Nothing painful, mind you, 'cuz I'm no sadist. Just that he be taken quietly, but taken. I did that every morning for twenty-five years."

Every morning. I didn't realize you were so devout.

"Sure I was. And you know what happened today at work? You know what sent shock waves through the plant?"

I can guess. Your prayers have been answered and your boss has finally . . .

"No. What happened was that he reached retirement age but he's staying on for five more years. And I'm not going to church any more."

Does this mean that your faith has been shaken, you no longer believe in God?

"Nah. It means that you don't have to worry about those hostile prayers because what happened to me has taught me a lesson in theology."

●   20

What lesson?

"That God don't listen to jerks."

War Is Heaven—
If You Believe

May 31, 1984

The punishment seems harsh for that young marine corporal from Chicago who wouldn't go to Lebanon because of his Moslem religious beliefs. He's been sentenced to four months of hard labor and a bad-conduct discharge.

On the other hand, a line has to be drawn somewhere. And whether or not Corporal Alfred Griffin realized it, he was trying to goof up the ancient rules and traditions of warfare.

He said that because he practices the Moslem religion, he could not kill another Moslem. And that's why he didn't show up when his outfit shipped out.

Well, what kind of attitude is that? If soldiers refused to kill somebody simply because they practice the same religion, it would be damned hard to get a war going.

Why, you don't see Iraq and Iran quibbling over questions of faith. They're all Moslems, and very devout. But with Allah's name on their lips, and their holy men urging them on, they've been eagerly slaughtering each other by the tens of thousands.

Nor have Christians ever been squeamish about waging wars on other Christians. If they had been, most of the liveliest wars in Europe would never have occurred.

Germany is loaded with Christians of all denominations. But every so often, it feels the need to shoot its way into France, Poland and other Christian nations. France, in its Napoleonic heyday, didn't hesitate to stomp all over other European Christians.

If anything, faith sometimes helped get their blood pressure pumped up, although it's doubtful that Christ intended His message to be used that way. Some wars were fought precisely over the issues of who prayed loudest, who ought to be leading the prayers, who kicked in the most loot to holy men and who should be admitted to heaven. The issues never stayed resolved for much longer than it took to count and stack the bodies of the faithful, but all the killing seemed like a good idea at the time.

If everybody thought the way that marine corporal does, World Wars I and II, which set records for Christians killing Christians, could never have occurred. Pilots and bombardiers and cannon-shooters would have been saying to themselves: "I wonder if any of my fellow Lutherans are down there?" Or: "I'll be darned—that guy I just shot crossed himself just the way I do just before he expired." Which is negative thinking of the worst kind.

Actually, there are benefits to waging war on people of the same faith.

For one thing, if you're taken prisoner and you die, you have a good chance of receiving a Christian burial, which is always nicer than being tossed out with the leftovers. And on religious holidays, the prison guards might be warmed by the spirit of the day and give you one less kick.

Also, both sides usually try to avoid destroying churches that have significant histories or architectural value. In Italy, for example, a lot of bystanders were killed, but a surprisingly large number of fine churches were undamaged. That's good because it means that there will be attractive settings available for the funerals of civilians who happen to be blown up.

●   22

When both sides have the same religion, it's reassuring to know that the other guy might not have a heavenly edge. Maybe the enemy's holy man is telling him the Lord is on his side, but since your holy man is assuring you of the same thing, the worst you figure to get is a draw.

Then again, there are advantages to fighting wars with people who have different beliefs. Some religions promise heavenly reward to those who zap nonbelievers. Most at least imply that it's a little less sinful to knock off somebody from an off-brand faith. And it does make for a more interesting variety of religious souvenirs and trinkets to be plucked from enemy corpses.

I have to suspect that the marine corporal has little knowledge of his own nation's history, which includes our own bloody Civil War, fought between people not only of the same faith, but of the same nation and, in some cases, the same families. That's the beauty of a civil war: Everybody has to put aside all those petty personal considerations for the overall social benefits of blowing somebody away.

All things considered, our present situation is probably the best arrangement, at least from the point of view of those who might think like the corporal, since the next big war would probably pit us—a religious nation—against the Soviets and godless Communism.

It could be the world's biggest and final opportunity to finally find out once and for all if God really takes sides in these differences.

Boy, if He doesn't, won't all those earlier holy warriors feel silly?

Padded Cell 1

"Gimme, Gimme!"

Even Darkest Day
Has a Bright Side

October 21, 1987

As the Dow Jones plunged on Black Monday, I nervously pondered the possibility of another Great Depression and wondered what I should do to survive.

So I phoned my wife and said: "Buy coal."

"Why should I buy coal?"

"Because when I was a kid during the Depression, if you had coal in the basement for the furnace, you were all right."

"But we have a gas furnace."

"Buy some coal anyway in case they turn off the gas. The utilities are heartless. And buy potatoes."

"Why?"

27 ●

"Because I remember that we ate a lot of potato pancakes. Cheap, and they stick to your ribs. And remember to switch off the lights."

But after we spoke, I turned on the TV and heard a financial expert say the stock plunge might merely be a long-overdue adjustment, and there is no reason to climb out on a window ledge.

Even more important, he said that this could be the time to take advantage of some shrewd buying opportunities.

Not wanting to miss any shrewd opportunities, I immediately headed for LaSalle Street, the heart of our city's financial district.

I saw a well-dressed young man stumbling along, holding his hands to his face and moaning.

"Excuse me," I said, "but can I ask you a personal question?"

"What is it?" he cried. "Make it quick, I'm heading for the nearest bridge."

"Are you a yuppie?"

"Yes, I am a devout yuppie."

"And you wouldn't happen to also be an MBA, would you?"

"To my lasting regret, yes."

"And are you a broker or a trader?"

"Yes, yes, but why are you asking me these questions."

"I just wondered what kind of watch you're wearing."

"A Rolex, of course. What kind of yuppie MBA broker-trader do you take me for?"

"Would you care to sell it?"

"Would I?" he cried, yanking it off and thrusting it at me.

I stuffed a few greenbacks in his hand and said: "Is that a Burberry trench coat you're wearing?"

"Yes, brand-new," he said, tearing it off. "You want it?"

"Deal. And I can't help but notice a Mont Blanc pen in your pocket. Would you . . ."

"Name your price and you've got it. I've already used it to write a farewell note to my sweetheart, an assistant aerobics instructor."

"Thank you. And what about that Hermès scarf and the Porsche designer sunglasses, hmmmm?"

"As you can see, the scarf is newly tearstained, so I'll knock off 10 percent."

"Make it 20. Now, let me ask what kind of wheels you have?"

He fell back against a wall as if stricken.

"You mean my . . ." And he began weeping.

"Is it a BMW?"

"Of course. Hand-washed every second day since I've owned it. Oh, my Bavarian beauty."

"I know how you must feel. But at a time like this, you really should consider divesting yourself of this asset. It is a drain on your cash flow."

He took the car keys from his pocket and said: "It has a list price of . . ."

I shook my head. "You don't understand. Now that the Dow has hit 1,700, the market is glutted with them."

I stuffed a few more bills into his hand and took the keys.

"Anything else?" I said.

"Well, there's my Olin skis, my Lotus Elan bike, and my espresso machine."

"Where are they?"

"At my condo."

"Ah, you have a condo. Lakefront, I assume?"

"Are there condos elsewhere?"

"I'm sure we can agree on a reasonable price, including the furnishings. Deal?"

"I have little choice."

"Fine. Have we missed anything?"

"Well, yes, there is my . . . my . . . no, I can't bring myself to part with it."

"Be realistic. What is it?"

"No, I can't, it's more precious to me than anything else."

"What is it, your home multimedia center? Your Kangaroo golf bag and all-graphite clubs? Your Prince racket? You can't take them with you."

"No, it's my . . . membership in the East Bank Club. With my own locker."

"Ah, poor devil. But I'll take it. And to show you I'm not without heart, I'll take you there one last time as my guest. Well, nice doing business with you. Bye."

"Wait," he said, as he searched through his pockets. Then he withdrew a small metal container.

"Here," he said. "You might as well have it all."

"What is it?"

"My coke," he said.

"No thanks. I prefer Pepsi."

Huh, Let Wall Street Run for Cover

December 7, 1987

On the first really cold day of this winter, I reached into the back of the closet for my heavy overcoat.

As I put it on, the wife made a retching sound and

said: "You're not going to wear that awful thing again, are you?"

Why not? It's warm and it fits. What more can I ask of a coat?

"It's old and filthy," she said. "Look in the mirror."

I looked at my reflection. True, some threads dangled from the bottom and the collar. And there were a few mud stains here and there. The cuffs were frayed and a couple of buttons were missing. But I pointed out that the basic structure was sound.

"You ought to throw it out and buy a new one," she said.

But it isn't really that old. I bought it in 1971.

"That's sixteen years," she said, sounding amazed.

Ah, but a coat isn't like a car. I wear it only during the winters. The rest of the year, it rests. So it's much younger than it looks.

"Please," she said, "I'm really embarrassed when we go someplace in public. I've seen coatroom attendants look sick when they have to handle it."

So as I went out the door, I agreed to buy a new overcoat, although the thought was painful. Not only am I sentimental about old clothes, I'm cheap. The coat's price had been $140, the most I ever spent on a garment. But by wearing it all those years, I had amortized—I think that's the word—the original cost down to about $9.31 a year. Or maybe $9.50 with dry cleaning.

But she was probably right, so I set off toward my favorite fashionable discount clothing store.

Just before I got there, though, the voice on my car radio said: "And in financial news, the Dow Jones average has plunged seventy-two points, with declining issues outnumbering advances five to one.

"Analysts say the latest decline was brought on by reports of sluggish sales in November."

31 ●

Then one of the analysts came on and mournfully talked about how nervous Wall Street was becoming because consumers aren't spending enough money.

And he said that if consumers didn't get out there and start spending money faster, this could lead to even more sharp dips, plunges, turbulence and gyrations in the market.

I suddenly realized that by purchasing a new coat, I would be doing a favor for those hysterics on Wall Street.

So I hit the brakes, made a U-turn, and looked down at my coat and said: "That's it, old pal, it's you and me for another year. I'm not going to cast you aside just to help those profit-grubbing fools."

Finally I have found a way to fight back against these madmen.

For several years now, they've been playing their crazy game, buying stocks for more than they can possibly be worth, pushing up the prices, selling, buying, merging, insider swapping, then running out to get a new Rolex.

Brokers have been persuading the gullible to buy stocks in companies about which they know nothing. They don't know if the chairman of the board is a lush, if the bookkeeper is stealing from petty cash or if the factory roof leaks and the toilets back up. They don't even know where the company is located or what the heck they make or sell.

Many of the companies weren't even making money. But that didn't stop Wall Street. Wild-eyed people listened to the brokers, the experts, the authors of financial newsletters, who shouted buy, buy, buy. And they threw more money at them and the prices went up.

Now it's all crashing down. If you read the *Wall Street Journal,* all you get is pitiful moaning. Story after story about brokers who are trembling, economists who are quaking, financiers who are standing in pools of sweat, investors who are down to their skivvies.

And that's the publication that calls itself the "diary of the American dream." Dream? It reads more like the diary of the delirium tremens.

So now, whom are they blaming for their own idiotic behavior? The consumers, because we're not spending enough. Me and my old coat.

I'm glad they told me because I'm going to do everything I can to keep them miserable. The coat stays. So do the frayed underwear, the gravy-stained ties, the round-heeled shoes.

For Christmas, I'll give the kids a promissory note for cash that I will put aside for them in an old coffee can in a corner of the basement. That way, they can't spend it, either.

And how will I benefit from this? Maybe this time next year, I can sell my old coat to some needy soul on Wall Street.

Opportunity Calls
a Wrong Number

July 12, 1988

In an aggressively cheerful voice, the caller said: "Mr. Royko? And how are you feeling this morning?"

I said: "Who are you and what do you want?"

That's the way I usually respond to bubbly people who phone and ask how I am feeling. How I'm feeling was none of his business, unless he was my physician, which he wasn't.

And I knew his question wasn't sincere. Strangers who call and ask how you are feeling really don't care.

33 ●

They almost always try to sell you something or put the arm on you for a favor.

So after I asked who he was and what he wanted, he said his name was David Roffman and he was a broker for a company called Blinder-Robinson.

Then he made his pitch. He said he would like to talk to me about some investment opportunities.

See? I told you he didn't really care how I was feeling.

But I was polite. Although he was interrupting me while I was trying to earn a living, I understood that he was just trying to earn a living.

So I thanked him for calling, but said I was not interested in pursuing any investment opportunities.

That should have been the end of the conversation, but he pushed forward, asking if I bought stocks, if I made investments, and if so, what kind?

Again, I politely but firmly told him that I was working, I was busy, and I was not interested in buying what he was selling. Then I said good-bye and hung up.

About three minutes later, my phone rang again. And once again it was David Roffman of Blinder-Robinson.

"We spoke earlier," he said.

Yes, we did. Three minutes ago. And three minutes ago I told you I wasn't interested. Why are you calling me again?

"Well, I thought you might want to reconsider."

After three minutes?

"Yes, I thought you might have given it further thought and I'd . . ."

Ah, I understood. You thought that during the three minutes that elapsed, I sat back in my chair and thought: *I have blown an opportunity to become rich!* If only I had listened to that David Roffman, I might be well on my way to Easy Street by now. He could be making me rich. So, are you going to *make me rich,* Mr. Roffman?

He said: "Ha-ha, well, I don't know if I can make you rich."

You don't? Have you made anyone rich, Mr. Roffman? Can you give me the names of people who will swear under oath that your financial wisdom has built their vast fortunes?

He said: "Ha-ha, well, I can't say that, but some of them have done well."

Mr. Roffman, how old are you?

"I'm twenty-four," he said.

You said twenty-four?

"Yes, I'm twenty-four."

Mr. Roffman, the day you were born, it's likely that I was doing what I'm doing today. Batting out a newspaper column and earning a decent living. My family had a sturdy roof over its head. We had food on our table. And our two dogs had food in their bowls. But do you know what has happened in those twenty-four years?

"What?"

I am still earning a decent living. My family still has a roof over its head. There is still food on the table and in the bowls, although the dogs have been replaced by cats. And do you know how I accomplished that?

"How?"

I did that by not being stupid enough to entrust my money to some twenty-four-year-old guy who calls me on the telephone out of the blue and asks me to let him play games with my dough.

He was silent, so I went on. At that point I may have been ranting.

Mr. Roffman, I read the *Wall Street Journal,* which, with a straight face, calls itself the diary of the American dream. And all I read about are financial jackals tearing at each other's throats. I read about takeovers, insider deals, poison pills, Chapter 11s, indictments, investigations, betrayals, back-stabbings, swindles, cons and guys like Ivan Boesky going to a country club prison. I read about computers that bounce stock values like a yo-yo. And you expect me to throw my helpless, defenseless money into that den of thieves and vipers? I would be better off going to Vegas, sitting down at a blackjack table, and taking hits all day on fifteen. Mr. Roffman, are you beginning to understand what my investment strategies are?

"Uh, you aren't interested."

Very good, Mr. Roffman. But don't feel bad. If you have a hot stock, you should call your ma, your pa, your sisters, brothers and friends and neighbors. Let them get rich. Share this golden opportunity with your loved ones. Why waste it on a stranger like me?

"I see," said Mr. Roffman. "Good-bye."

I waited three minutes. The phone didn't ring. Too bad. I never did get a chance to tell him how I was feeling that morning.

Going-for-Broke
Justice for Hunts

September 5, 1986

One of the strangest people I've met as part of my job was H. L. Hunt, the oil tycoon who was once considered the world's wealthiest man.

In his twilight years, Hunt, who seldom spoke to reporters, would call me when he visited Chicago and volunteer to be interviewed.

It wasn't clear why he wanted to talk to me, although I wondered if he planned to convert me to his way of thinking, which was so far right that he made Barry Gold-water sound like a pinko.

For example, one of his pet political theories was that a person should cast as many votes as he had dollars.

That, of course, would put the selection of presidents and Congress in the hands of a few billionaires like Hunt, which he thought was only fair. He didn't see any logic in a guy who was broke casting a vote.

We'd sit in his hotel suite, sipping Cokes—he shunned liquor—while he reminisced about how he had started as a young poker shark in southern Illinois, bought Texas oil leases and wheeled and dealed his way to billions.

Sometimes he sang. That's right, sang. He had written and published an awful novel about his ideal society—where the rich had the votes—and he composed a song to go with it.

He would sing in an off-key, reedy voice, bobbing his head to achieve a tremolo. An audience of one, I'd listen to one of the world's richest men tweeting like a plump-faced bird.

I even took him on a radio news show I used to do in the morning. The co-host, said: "Who's this?" I said: "H. L. Hunt, the richest man in America. He is going to sing for our audience."

And Hunt did. About a dozen listeners promptly phoned to ask if their radios were malfunctioning or if we had gone nuts.

I never was sure what to write about Hunt after our interviews, other than he was quite the oddball. This didn't bother him, but he took offense when I wrote that he wore a cheap suit. He mailed me a tailor's receipt for $800. I wrote back that I might become a tailor.

Hunt is now gone. He died in 1974, leaving most of his billions to a horde of children he sired by four wives. He was, incidentally, a bigamist. When you have that kind of money, who bothers with minor, legal details?

And today I can't help laughing when I think about Hunt and his political theories, and the plight that his three most famous sons are in.

As you probably have read, a bunch of banks are suing the Hunt brothers—Lamar, Nelson and Herbert—for more than $770 million in unpaid loans.

They got in hock for this incredible sum because their greed boiled over a few years ago. Already billionaires, they secretly tried to corner the world silver market, figuring they could drive up the price, sell and pick up a few billion more.

But before they completed the scheme, silver prices slumped and they wound up losing a few billion instead.

So they had to go to several banks and ask for a billion-dollar loan to cover their losses.

If you've dealt with banks, you might think that would be an impossible request. Some working stiffs can't persuade banks to lend them the price of a new siding job for the three-flat.

But banks are eager to please customers like the Hunt brothers. What's the problem, boys? You tried to corner the world silver supply and got caught? Hey, no problem. How many hundred million you need?

Now the banks are upset because the Hunts aren't keeping up with their payments. And they're trying to grab some of the Hunt oil companies.

Being labeled as deadbeats might embarrass some people. But the Hunts were indignant. They turned around and sued the banks for suing them and have asked for billions in damages. The rest of us might think about that route—not making the mortgage payments, then suing the bank for being pesty.

The Hunts have also tried to avoid losing their main stash by placing much of it under bankruptcy court protection.

The high-priced lawyers and federal judges will have to thrash out who owes what to whom. And the nice thing about this drama is that no matter who loses—the Hunts or the banks—they probably deserve it.

But if the Hunts are eventually wiped out, as some financial experts predict, it might cause me to rethink my opinion of old H. L.'s political ideas.

In the old man's perfect society, anybody without assets who showed up to vote would be given the bum's rush. If they go broke, that will be the fate of Lamar, Nelson and Herbert.

Maybe the old man had something after all.

Some Cars
Make Dumb Statements

October 25, 1988

Although I've never met Frederick J. Schwab, I must assume that he's a big heat in his line of work.

His stationery says he is senior executive vice president of Porsche Cars North America Inc.

I know this because he has sent me a personal invitation to drive one of his Porsche cars. And maybe buy one.

In a burst of enthusiasm, he wrote:

"Imagine yourself behind the wheel of one of the most powerful and exciting automotive machines in the world—a new Porsche 928 S4."

I did as he suggested. I closed my eyes and imagined myself behind the wheel of a Porsche 928 S4.

The imaginary vision didn't do much for me. I could hear my wife saying, as she always does: "Do you mind not smoking in the car?"

39

Then I saw myself pulling into the madness of the expressway, being wedged between a giant truck and a '69 Pontiac belching black fumes, and everybody slowing to five miles an hour to gape at a family of twelve, who share twenty teeth, standing on the shoulder of the road pondering a flat tire on their pickup truck.

As fantasies go, it wasn't much fun, so I opened my eyes and went on with Vice President Schwab's letter.

"We've got one with your name on it, and I want to personally invite you to your local Porsche dealer for a complimentary test drive.

"Come and experience the incomparable handling, the smooth power, the pure excitement of driving this exceptional automobile. Sit behind the wheel and surround yourself with the sleek styling that made Porsche famous.

"However, one word of caution: After you drive a new Porsche 928 S4, you may be compelled to own one."

No, Mr. Schwab, you're mistaken. I will not be compelled to own one.

After receiving your invitation, I called a Porsche dealer and asked how much your 928 S4 doodad costs. He said between $74,000 and $80,000 depending on what accessories I wanted in it.

I told him that for $74,000 to $80,000 the least I would expect to find in it would be a couple of gorgeous German dollies. The stiff said those were not the kinds of accessories they dealt in. Well, if they did, Mr. Schwab wouldn't have to resort to sending letters to the likes of me.

In any case, he couldn't have picked a less likely prospect.

Not that I'm cheap, but I consider $75,000 to $80,000 a bit steep for a car—even one with "incomparable handling" and "smooth power."

How much incomparable handling and smooth power does one need to get around Chicago? The secrets of survival are to get out of the way of interstate trucks, remember that Friday is drunk-driving night on the expressways and never give the finger to someone with a tattoo on his arm who is driving a clunker that looks uninsurable.

And while I don't want to criticize Mr. Schwab's product, frankly, I don't see where they get off charging $80,000 for something that small.

If I was going to throw that kind of money around, I would want something long and flashy—an old-time, fat, bloated, Detroit gas-guzzler. Then, with a big cigar clenched between my teeth and a pinky ring on my finger, I could pass for an alderman or a Mafia elder and get some respect.

But in a Porsche, people would justifiably assume that I was a yuppie who trades pork bellies or soybean futures, since those are the sort of people who buy Porsches. Who needs that kind of humiliation?

As students of the auto industry tell us, once you pass a certain prudent, sensible limit in car buying, you are no longer just buying transportation.

You are making a statement.

My cars have always made a statement. They are covered with bird droppings, soot, grime, salt. The inside is littered with ashes, grimy coffee cups, old newspapers, crumpled candy wrappers and letters I forgot to drop at the corner mailbox.

The statement my cars make is: "Modern life requires that I own one of these things, but I don't have to like it."

But if I bought one of Mr. Schwab's trinkets, I would be making an entirely different statement.

I would be telling the world: "Look, everybody, I have paid $80,000 for a small car that is capable of going 150 miles an hour, although the speed limit is 35 where I do most of my driving. And if I leave it unattended on a city street for more than two minutes, the car thieves will have a tag team match over who gets to steal it. Therefore, the statement I am making with this car is: 'I am a real jerk.' "

Finally, Mr. Schwab, I have to tell you that I cannot buy your car because it is not made in this country. I don't buy cars made in Germany or Japan.

I'm not spiteful, and I believe in letting bygones be bygones. But I have a personal policy of waiting a hundred years between wars before doing business.

Write me again in 2045.

Shortage of Short Greeks Ruining Us

December 5, 1986

The moment we sat down for lunch, I knew it was a mistake. It was one of those cute new yuppie-poo restaurants with ferns and a menu that listed calories.

I knew it was an even bigger mistake when five minutes passed before the busboy dropped the silverware and napkins in front of us.

About ten minutes later, I snared a waitress as she was hurrying by and asked: "Is there any chance we can see a menu?"

She flung down a couple of menus and rushed off. About five minutes later, she was back for the orders.

"I'm so sorry," she said. "We're short-handed. One of the girls didn't show up today."

When she finally brought the food, it wasn't what I had ordered.

"There are some problems in the kitchen," she said. "We have a new cook."

●   42

"Never mind," I said. "I'll eat it, whatever it is. But what about the beer?"

"Oh, I forgot, you wanted a beer," she said. The beer arrived just in time to wash down the last bite of the sandwich.

When she brought the check, which was wrong because she charged me for what I ordered instead of what I got, I asked: "Who runs this place?"

"The manager?" she said. "He's in the end booth having lunch."

On the way out, I stopped at the manager's booth. He was a yuppie in a business suit. He and a clone were leisurely sipping their coffee and looking at a computer printout.

"Nice place you have here," I lied. "Do you own it?"

The young man shook his head. It was owned by one of those big corporations that operate restaurants in far-flung office buildings and health clubs.

He also proudly told me that he had recently left college with a degree in restaurant and hotel management.

That explained it all. His waitresses were short-handed, his cook was goofing up the orders, the customers were fuming and what was he doing?

He was having lunch. Or, as he'd probably say, he was *doing* lunch.

I don't want to be an alarmist, but when this nation collapses, he and those like him will be the cause.

First, we had the MBA—especially the Harvard MBA—who came along after World War II and took over American industry. With his bottom-line approach, the MBA did such a brilliant job that the Japanese might soon buy the whole country and evict us.

But we're told not to worry. Now that we don't manufacture as much as we used to, we'll be saved by the growing service industry.

43 ●

The problem is that the service industry is being taken over by people like the restaurant manager and his corporation. They go to college and study service. Then they install computers programmed for service. And they have meetings and look at service charts and graphs and talk about service.

But what they don't do is provide service. That's because they are not short Greeks.

You probably wonder what that means. I'll explain.

If that corporation expects the restaurant to succeed, it should fire the young restaurant-hotel degree holder. Or demote him to cleaning washrooms.

It should then go to my friend Sam Sianis, who owns Billy Goat's Tavern, and say: "Do you know a short Greek who wants to manage a restaurant?"

Sam will say: "Shoo. I send you one my cousins. Jus' got here from old country."

Then he'd go to Greek Town and tell his cousin, who works as a waiter, that his big chance had come.

When the next lunch hour rolled around, and a waitress failed to show up for work, Sam's cousin would not sit down to do lunch. He would put on an apron and wait tables himself.

If the cook goofed up orders, Sam's cousin would go in the kitchen, pick up a cleaver and say, "You want I keel you?"

He wouldn't know how to read a computer printout, but he'd get drinks in the glasses, food on the table and money in the cash register.

That simple approach is why restaurants run by short Greeks stay in business and make money. And why restaurants that are run by corporations and managed by young men who are educated beyond their intelligence come and go. And mostly go.

So if you are ever approached by a stockholder who wants to sell you shares in any of the giant service corporations, tell him not to bother showing you the annual report. Just ask him one question.

"Is it run by short Greeks?"

If he says no, leave your money under the mattress.

Padded Cell 2

"Lifestyles of the Who?"

When "Prix Fixe" Is
Hard to Swallow

June 27, 1988

While browsing through a restaurant directory, I suggested to the blonde that we might try a place that was newly listed.

She asked if it was expensive and I said that it had a "prix fixe" dinner.

"A *what?*" she said.

I repeated, "Prix fixe."

"How is it spelled?"

I spelled it aloud and again said: "Prix fixe."

"You're not pronouncing it correctly," she said.

Why not? I'm pronouncing it exactly the way it is spelled.

"No, no. If you say it that way, it sounds, well, it sounds obscene."

I said it again: "Prix fixe," the way it is spelled. And she may be right. It did sound like it might be a phrase describing some sort of male surgical procedure.

"The proper pronunciation," the blonde said, flaunting her refined upbringing, "is pree feeks."

Then why isn't it spelled pree feeks?

"Because it is French. And in French, pree feeks is spelled 'prix fixe.' "

How stupid of me. I had forgotten that the first rule of the French language is that almost nothing is pronounced the way it's spelled. When the French invented their language, they rigged it that way just to make the rest of us feel inferior. They also thought that if they had a language that was almost impossible to learn, the Germans might not invade them.

"Pree feeks," the blonde said. "It simply means fixed price."

I already knew that much. The question is, why do newspaper and magazine restaurant listings in the United States, where most of us speak one form of English or another, insist on using "prix fixe," which is pronounced "pree feeks" and means "fixed price," instead of "fixed price," which means fixed price and is pronounced "fixed price"?

My guess is that the vast majority of Americans do not know how to pronounce "prix fixe." And a great many don't even know what it means.

Why, if you went into some restaurants in Arkansas or Tennessee and asked if they had a "prix fixe" dinner— pronouncing it the way it is spelled—it's likely that the waiter would bellow, "Ya lowdown preevert," and hit you with a catfish.

My newspaper, I'm sorry to say, is no exception. We have "prix fixes" scattered all through our restaurant listings. I asked a few copy editors, who are experts in such matters, why we don't just say "fixed price." They weren't sure.

One of them said that he thought we did it when reviewing French restaurants.

If so, we're being inconsistent. We may even be discriminating.

For example, when we list a German restaurant, we don't say "fester preis," which is German for fixed price.

Fester preis. It has a pleasant, homey ring. It sounds like the name of somebody who lives deep in the Ozarks. "Howdy, I'm Fester Preis and this here is my brother Lester Preis and my uncle Chester Preis."

In our listings for Chinese restaurants, we don't write "Gu din jia ge," which I was told by a Chinese acquaintance means "fixed price." Of course, he might have been pulling my leg. For all I know, it means: "The person who wrote this column is a geek." But I'll take his word for it.

I was going to include the Greek version of "fixed price," but Sam Sianis, who owns Billy Goat's Tavern, said: "Feex price? You crazy? In Greek joints, we no got feex price. We charge what we can get."

Another copy editor told me that "prix fixe" is used so widely that it had become the accepted, common meaning for "fixed price."

That didn't make sense to me, either. I've never picked up the financial pages and read a story that said:

"Three steel companies have been accused by the antitrust division of the Justice Department of prix fixing. The companies engaged in the fixe, sources say, to drive up the prix of steel."

Years ago, when Chicago was strictly a meat-and-potatoes town, we didn't have such linguistic problems.

I suppose that as we became more sophisticated, this was the prix we paid.

51 ●

Shopping
Isn't Everyone's Bag

October 5, 1988

I still haven't figured out why it is such a big deal that Bloomingdale's, the New York department store, has opened a branch in Chicago.

The newspapers, TV stations and disc jockeys have become giddy over the arrival of the store.

And the silliness may have peaked when a gushy female reporter from the *New York Times* called and asked me to describe my own excitement.

I explained to her that while certain activities excite me, most of which I would not describe to a respectable woman, the opening of a Bloomingdale's store is not one of them.

Furthermore, I said, this is not Wyoming. We already have enough famous, high-priced stores in Chicago to satisfy the self-indulgence of every coke-sniffing pork-belly trader in town, as well as their wives, mistresses or any other sex objects of their choice.

Not easily discouraged, the New York reporter asked: "Are you going to go shop at Bloomingdale's?"

"No," I said.

"Why not?"

"Because I don't shop."

"Everybody shops," she said.

"Not me. I do not shop."

"Then how do you get your clothes?"

An interesting question. So I explained.

About five years ago, I was in my closet looking for something to wear that didn't have gravy stains on the lapels.

As I searched the cluttered room, I realized that I had

enough garments and shoes to open a men's shop.

That's because I never throw any clothes away. I have suits, shoes, jackets, slacks and shirts that are more than twenty-five years old.

Some of the trousers are worn thin in the seat. But if you wear shorts that match the trouser color, few will notice. And many of the jacket sleeves have holes at the elbows. But you can get a leather patch sewn on for a few bucks, then pose as a professor of literature.

Most of the shoes have holes in the bottom. But in dry weather it doesn't matter. And for winter I have Luigi, my neighborhood shoemaker, give a few pairs a rehab.

As I went through this ancient but vast wardrobe, counting each item, digging some out from under old luggage, something remarkable occurred to me.

After making a count, I called an actuary and asked him how long I could expect to live. He said that based on my personal habits, a few minutes or maybe an hour. But based on his statistical tables, a few more decades.

I did mental calculations: How many shirts per year, how many shoes, how many slacks, sweaters, jackets and so on.

And I realized that if I lived to a ripe, even rancid, old age, I would never again have to buy another garment.

I even set aside my least shiny suit and a shirt with a sturdy collar button to be buried in. (However, that won't be necessary because I have since redone my will, instructing my wife to stuff my remains in a Hefty bag and call the ward sanitation superintendent for a special pickup.)

One of the benefits of having all these old clothes is that every couple of years, some of them come back in style. If I could find my original zoot suit, bought when I was seventeen from Smokey Joe's on Halsted Street, I'd be a sensation in the Hard Rock Cafe.

On the other hand, one of the disadvantages is that

I frequently look like a bum. However, there are advantages to that disadvantage. For one thing, if you look as rumpled and frayed as I usually do, you're less likely to be mugged. In fact, when I walk on a street, people who see me approaching sometimes cross to the other side, fearing I might mug them.

Anyway, I explained all this to the New York reporter. Being clever, she said: "Yes, but what about socks and undergarments? You have to shop for them."

Not so. My wife buys them for me, although my favorite brands are becoming harder to find with the decline of Army-Navy Surplus stores.

Sounding amazed, the reporter said: "You're the first person I've ever talked to who never shops. I can't believe it."

So I told her that I wasn't being entirely truthful. I admitted that I sometimes make purchases at a Salvation Army resale shop.

"Ah," the reporter said, "you do shop after all."

Of course, I said, I have loved ones, and I have to get them something for Christmas and birthdays. I'm no Scrooge.

A Critical Look
at Contact Lenses

October 28, 1985

He was bent over a sink in the office men's room, poking a finger into his eye and muttering.

I asked him what his problem was.

"The air. Must be a lot of pollution or something. It goofs up my contact lenses."

● 54

No, I scoffed, his problem wasn't the air. His problem was the vanity of those who insist on wearing contact lenses because they think it makes them look better and conceals a minor physical flaw.

They can't be like the rest of us normal, well-balanced, weak-eyed people who are not embarrassed about perching regular glasses on our noses.

They are so concerned about their appearance, so lacking in self-confidence, so vain and filled with conceit, that they go to the trouble of sticking a tiny piece of plastic to their eyeballs.

While poking at his eye, he indignantly offered a long, lame explanation about how much better he can see with contacts.

I've heard it before. But there is only one reason to wear them, and it is vanity.

I used to hear the same stuff from the right fielder on my softball team every time we had to stop the game while he crawled around on all fours, looking in the grass for a lens that had somehow leaped from his eyeball.

And I used to hear it from a handball partner, as he crawled on all fours, peering into the cracks between the floorboards.

There is also the golf partner, who in the midst of a game will suddenly clap his hand over an eye or begin poking at the orb with a finger.

That's the most offensive part of it—when they stick fingers in their own eyes.

Never once in my entire life have I touched either of my own eyeballs. Nor have I permitted anyone to touch them.

And I never will. To touch the eye is against the laws of nature. No creature on earth wants its eyeball touched.

You can make a test to confirm that statement. Take the nicest, gentlest cat you can find. Or the most docile, tail-wagging, droolingly happy dog.

You can pet them. You can rub their ears. You can ruffle the fur under their necks. You might even be able to get away with pulling their tails.

But just dare to try to touch their eyes. Those friendly little beasts might nip off your finger, as they should.

Or try it with a friend. You can pat a friend's back, put a hand on a friend's shoulder, take a friend by the arm, even pat a friend on the cheek.

But make the test. Go up to any friend, even your best pal, and try to touch his or her eyeball. They will leap away.

And it isn't mere surprise that causes that reaction. Give them warning. Ask your friend, "Would you mind if I touch your eyeball with my finger?"

You do that once or twice and your friends will shun you.

There is also the inconvenience. People who wear those things can't just yank off their glasses and toss them on the dresser or under the bed when they go to sleep.

They have to mess around with their eyes to remove them, put them in a miniature cooker, simmer them or whatever they do overnight, then go through the whole thing again in the morning.

And we've all heard the stories about people who awake thirsty during the night and, in reaching for a glass of water on the nightstand, accidentally drink their contact lens.

There is something else they can't do. When provoked in, say, a barroom debate, they can't make the menacing gesture of removing their glasses, putting them on the bar and serving notice that the talking is over. Now there is action.

A person would look pretty foolish saying "I don't have to put up with your guff" and then begin poking himself in the eye.

Finally, I have long suspected that there is a potential

health menace in contact lenses. Eye doctors will deny it. But logic tells me it exists.

The danger is this: What is to prevent those things from sliding off your eye and up behind your forehead and even farther up, into your cranium? What do you do then, when this tiny object is up there in your head, rattling around between your skull and your brain?

Think about that. And be careful about rolling your eyes.

If It Tastes Bad, Fatty, Eat It Up

May 11, 1984

A fat actor has written the latest best-selling diet book about how he shed excess blubber. If you are overweight, you might be tempted to buy it. Don't waste your money.

Like many of the popular diet books—and there's always one on the best-seller lists—it's basically a ripoff.

That's because the author tries to convince tubby people that they can lose weight while still enjoying tasty, delicious, yummy, satisfying meals.

It can't be done. I've read all kinds of diet books because, like most self-indulgent Americans, I've spent much of my adult life overweight.

I've tried the old-drinking-man's diet, the eat-anything-you-want diet, the three-squares-a-day diet, the lotsa-spicy-meatballs diet, the gobble-pasta-till-you-burst diet and all the other enjoy-eating-and-lose-weight diets.

No matter what they claim, there is only one diet that works.

I call it: The-You-Gotta-Suffer Diet.

Having just lost twenty-five pounds in about ten weeks, I know it works and I'm willing to share it with you. It's quite simple. You don't have to do a lot of calorie counting, measuring and weighing tiny bits of food or poring over time-consuming recipes.

All you have to do is be miserable, which is fundamental to any successful diet. And you have to remember only one rule, the cornerstone of my diet.

The rule is: If you enjoy it, you can't have it; if you don't like it, you can eat all you want.

This rule derives from the scientifically acknowledged fact that Mother Nature is a nasty, sadistic, mean broad. She made everything that tastes good fattening. And everything that is not fattening tastes terrible.

An example is the Brussels sprout. Under my diet, you can eat all the Brussels sprouts you want. Stuff yourself with them. Shove them in your mouth with both hands. You won't gain an ounce.

That's because Brussels sprouts are awful. Just as lettuce, celery, cabbage, carrots and most vegetables are awful.

The only vegetable that isn't awful is the potato—and only when it is french fried. Or baked and heaped with butter, sour cream and chunks of bacon. Or covered with gooey cheese. Then the potato tastes great. Therefore, you can't eat it.

See how simple it is?

Let's say you go to a German restaurant. There's no big problem in ordering low-calorie foods. You just order the worst thing on the menu.

The menu might have a pork shank with dumplings, which is great cuisine. So, you can't order it.

Order the broiled white fish, with some sliced tomatoes on the side. It's enough to make me gag.

When the waiter asks you what you will drink, follow the suffering rule. The best thing to drink would be a liter of German beer. The only thing better would be two liters of German beer. So you can't order it.

Instead, you order the worst thing the bar serves: a diet pop. Or, if you are stupid as well as overweight, Perrier with a twist.

Then comes dessert. You probably want something wonderful, like a big slab of cheesecake or some kind of rich chocolate cake.

Which means you can't have it. Instead, you must suffer and ask if they have any fresh melon. Squirt a bit of lemon juice on it, smile and pretend you are having a fine time, while you are ready to scream and do violence.

Or maybe you choose an Italian restaurant. Once again, the choice is not difficult. The best thing on the menu would probably be a plate of fettucine Alfredo, or spaghetti carbonara or lasagna. With a bottle or two of red wine. And a snort of anisette with your coffee.

So you order the baked halibut. With Tab.

The rule applies day and night, every meal, every snack.

Breakfast? Don't eat anything good, such as pancakes with sausage, French toast with bacon or hash with eggs. Eat miserable stuff, like half a bowl of oatmeal and some fruit juice. Achh!

Evening snacks? The best snacks known to civilized man are a big bowl of ice cream or half a pizza or two peanut butter and jelly sandwiches or a giant-sized bag of potato chips and a six-pack of beer. If you are a good American and a decent human being, you love these things.

So you can't have them. Eat some yogurt instead. Ugh.

That's it. When you go shopping, just walk down the supermarket aisle. If something makes you salivate, don't put it in your cart. If something makes you nauseated, take six of them.

Just follow the simple rule of suffering and misery and you'll lose weight. And, possibly, your mind.

On the Dull Edge
of Men's Fashion

July 28, 1986

Because he's a friend, I was concerned about his appearance and thought I should say something.

"Are you okay?" I asked.

"Sure, I'm fine."

"You're not working too hard, are you?"

"No more than usual. Why do you ask?"

"Just wondering. Look, can I ask you something personal?"

"Sure."

"Have you been drinking too much?"

"Of course not. Hey, what's this about?"

"I have to be frank. You've been looking seedy lately. You look like a bum."

"A bum? Oh, you mean this?"

He ran his hand across his chin.

"Yeah. You look like you haven't shaved for a couple of days. You've looked that way the last few times I've seen you."

He shook his head and said: "You really don't keep up with things, do you?"

"Well, I try to. Keeping up is part of my job."

"This is the look," he said.

"What look? You have a stubble beard."

Then he explained, and I felt foolish because I remembered that I had read something about it.

● 60

The stubble beard, giving him the appearance of a bum or a barfly, is fashionable. It's popularity stems from a weekly television police show, which I have managed never to see.

And since he is an unmarried yuppie, it is almost mandatory for him to follow such trends of fashion. He owes it to his socioeconomic class.

Once I understood, I said: "I get it. You only shave once a week or so?"

He shook his head. "Of course not. I shave every day."

"But if you shaved every day, you wouldn't look like a bum. Excuse me, I meant that you wouldn't be fashionable."

"I shave every day," he said. "Let me show you the secret."

From his briefcase, he withdrew an electric razor.

"It's terrific," he said. "It has two settings. One setting leaves just enough beard so I would have a one-day five o'clock shadow, if that's what I wanted."

"You have more than a five o'clock shadow," I said.

"Right. That's because it has another setting that leaves a five-day stubble, which is what I prefer."

"Amazing. Can I try it?"

I ran it across my chin, which I had shaved that morning. And he was right. Nothing happened. It didn't shave me.

"See?" he said. "But if you go five days without shaving, as I did, then use this every day, you'll always look like you have gone five days without shaving. It will just snip off the tiniest amount to achieve that effect."

And once again, I was in awe of the age we live in, with all of its technological marvels.

The genius of man has created a battery-operated razor that doesn't shave you.

"What does it cost?"

"About $30."

Remarkable. A razor that doesn't shave you for only $30.

It makes me wonder about other marketing opportunities.

If they can sell a razor that doesn't shave, why not an underarm deodorant that doesn't completely deodorize?

For the today kind of guy who wants just that subtle touch of manly grunginess.

I think something like that would sell. I think just about anything can sell.

If we don't run out of goofs.

Oh, the Hangups
That Phones Create

September 22, 1987

A man named Kent, who works for Motorola, was nice enough to send me a note about one of the company's space-age products.

"You know the importance of deadlines," Kent said, "and the importance of being able to be in immediate contact with people and they with you.

"Consider a Motorola factory direct mobile or portable cellular telephone (or a combination of the two).

"Do you carry a pager? Why, when you can easily carry a phone?

"Take it to work, to play, to lunch and still keep up with your customers, your suppliers, your life."

And he invited me to phone him so we could talk at greater length about this wondrous device.

I have to admit that I am a wondrous-device freak. I

have a wristwatch that is a combination calculator, data bank, stopwatch and alarm clock. I have an electronic gizmo that tells me if there is a fish under my boat. I have a car with buttons that tell me how long I've been gone and when I can expect to get where I'm going and when I'll get back. I have a personal computer that has a button I hit to find out if I have any money left after buying so many wondrous devices.

However, I'm not going to call Kent from Motorola because if there is one wondrous device I don't want, it is a portable telephone.

Sure, I know the importance, as Kent said, "of being able to be in immediate contact with people and they with you."

But I know something of greater importance—being able to hide from people. And to do that, you must maintain a safe distance from telephones.

I hate telephones. I have one in my office only because it's necessary for my work. I have one at home only because I can't order out for pizza without it.

Life was better before telephones became common. Back then, if some nuisance wanted to say something stupid to you, he had to sit down and write a letter or get on a streetcar and ride several miles to your home.

This took considerable effort. And there were defenses. Even today, if someone rings my doorbell, I can peek through a hole in the door and see who it is. If it's someone I don't want to talk to—which would include about 99 percent of the human race—I just remain silent and eventually the intruder goes away. He might ring the bell one more time, but that's about it.

But now, because of the telephone, all he has to do is hit seven numbers and he can come crashing into your life. He can keep ringing dozens of times. Or call back every five minutes.

The only defense is that truly humane device—the

recorded-message machine. Naturally, I own one. And I don't care who knows it—when my voice says: "Hi, I'm not in now . . ." I'm lying. I'm probably there, but I don't want to talk to you. If I did, I'd have called you in the first place.

That's the kind of message I wanted to put on when I first got the answering machine: "I'm right here, but I don't want to talk to you. And please don't leave a message. Send a brief postcard." But my wife wouldn't let me, the wimpette.

And Kent from Motorola wants to make a phone my constant companion?

Consider just one terrible consequence of owning a portable telephone and people knowing your number and being able to make immediate contact.

You are sitting in a bar after work, rewarding your frayed nerves for having earned another day's pay.

Suddenly your portable phone rings. You answer it and the familiar voice says: "I was about to put dinner on. Are you on the expressway?"

"Yes, yes, that's where I am, on the expressway, but traffic is terrible. Must be a big accident up ahead."

"What's that noise?"

"What noise?"

"All those voices. I thought I heard someone shout 'Bartender, another round.' "

"Oh, that? Yes, traffic is so jammed up that drivers are leaning out of windows and shouting things like 'We'd better go around.' "

"I hear a jukebox."

"That's my car radio."

"Turn it down."

"I can't, it's jammed."

"Are you really on the expressway?"

"I can't hear you, we have a bad connection."

"You *aren't* on the expressway."

"Hello, hello, I can't hear you. Good-bye."

Life is so less complicated, relationships are so much more stable if the bartender answers his phone and simply says: "No, he ain't been in this year."

So I wish Motorola or someone would invent the kind of phone I've been yearning for.

It would work this way. It would have a little screen on it. And after one ring, the screen would show the name of the person making the call. It would also have a button. And when I pressed the button, the caller's phone would emit an ear-shattering obscenity.

Call me, Kent, when you put that on the market. Better yet, drop me a brief postcard.

Yuppie Puppies
Having Their Day

March 21, 1985

Every so often, I see a tiny lady in my neighborhood walking her two big dogs. Actually, she doesn't walk them. She just hangs on to their chains and they sort of drag her along. Her feet appear to barely touch the ground.

Then it occurred to me that they were identical, so it was unlikely that they were mixed breeds, unless they came from the same litter.

So one day, as one of the dogs paused at the curb to moisten a subcompact auto, I asked the woman what kind of beasts they were.

"Akita," she said.

Ah, an Akita. What the heck is that?

"Japanese."

So the clever devils make dogs, too, eh? Do they have microchips?

"Stick your hand in their mouths and find out," she said a bit snippily as they all loped away.

That was the first I had heard of the Japanese exporting their dogs to us, too.

But now I have learned that this particular breed has become the most "in" dog in America. At least among those who choose their dogs on the basis of status. Namely, the yuppies.

According to *Success Magazine,* which knows about such things, the Akitas are so popular among yuppies that the dogs are often called "yuppie puppies." Ain't that cute?

Because I like to keep up with trends, I asked a local animal store owner about the Akita.

"Yeah, they're real popular now. I don't have any, but you see ads for them in all the dog magazines. I think the cheapest you can get one for is about $500. They can sell for $2,000 or $3,000 or even more."

What makes them so valuable?

"Because people want them and are dumb enough to pay the price. To me, they look something like an overweight German shepherd."

Can they do anything special?

"They bark. They growl. They're like any other dogs. If it's a decent pup to begin with, and you train it right, you'll have a good dog. If you don't train it right, you're going to have a $2,000 dog grabbing food off your plate, dumping on your rug and biting the mailman. Oh, and there's one other thing about them. The people who breed them say that at one time they were used to guard the Japanese emperor."

I thought that the Japanese emperor was guarded by samurai warriors—little bowlegged guys in diapers who grunt a lot.

"I don't know. Maybe they walked the dogs for the emperor. But it's part of the mystique."

Well, I'm not impressed. For that kind of money, a dog ought to be able to do something besides guard one Japanese emperor.

Take the St. Bernard, which you don't see too often. Many fastidious people don't like them because they are one of the breeds of dogs known as the Droolers.

But the St. Bernards have a great history. With that keg of brandy strapped under their chins, they used to go into the Alps and find travelers stranded in the snow. You're shivering in the cold and along comes a dog to offer you a pop of good hooch. Now, that's a man's best pal.

Guarding an emperor is mildly interesting, but no Japanese dog can compare to the noblest and most efficient of all guard dogs—the Chicago Tavern Dog.

As I've said before, the true Chicago Tavern Dog has to know whom to bite and whom not to bite—which isn't easy on a wild payday night, with people flying or falling every which way.

How would an emperor's $2,000 guard dog react if a dozen people were dancing a polka around him while somebody kicked the jukebox, somebody else threw a half-eaten sandwich at the TV, somebody was banging on the washroom door to wake up the occupant and a customer and the owner's wife were arm-wrestling for a round of drinks?

The mutt would probably have a nervous breakdown. Or, in the tradition of his homeland, throw himself on a corkscrew to end it all.

So when I see one of these $2,000 imports doing a job that many a $5 mongrel has done, I'll be impressed.

It might happen. With all the new yuppie fern bars, somebody will probably get a yuppie puppie and turn him into a tavern dog.

But I know what the result will be. Chicago thieves aren't dummies. They'll leave the ferns and steal the $2,000 dog.

All they'll have to do is offer him a bit of sushi.

Long and Short of Men's Fashion

November 19, 1984

When my grandfather sat on the front steps wearing his long underwear tops and drinking beer, it never occurred to me that he was a fashion trendsetter.

That was just the way he and his friends dressed. For more formal occasions, such as going to work or to Bruno's Corner Tap, they would slip a shirt and trousers over their long underwear.

For leisure-time activities, such as lounging on the front steps, they would remove the shirt.

And for those private, intimate moments, such as going to bed, they would remove the trousers but retain the long underwear.

When I asked him once why he wore long underwear on all but the hottest summer days, he said:

"Because wearing is what underwear is for."

But why, I asked, didn't he wear something lighter, such as briefs and a T-shirt.

He responded: "I'm no Italian gigolo."

But how does it look for you to be sitting around on the front steps in your underwear tops?

He explained. "When I got a shirt on, it's underwear. When I take my shirt off, it's not underwear any more because it's not under anything."

And he was true to his dress code throughout his life. Especially after the fire.

It happened in the middle of the night. A fire broke out in the basement, and smoke quickly seeped through the floors into his part of the three-flat.

As the firemen arrived he staggered out of the smoky building. Naturally, he was wearing his long underwear.

And he pointed triumphantly at the guy from the second floor, wrapped in a blanket because he had been wearing only briefs.

"See?" he said. "Don't Chester look funny?"

Now, it turns out, he was not only practical but fashionable.

I happened to come across a copy of a men's fashion magazine called *International Male*.

And as a picture in that magazine shows, one of the hottest new men's fashion items is "The Greek Undershirt."

As the magazine said: "We found this authentic Greek undershirt in Athens. The European fashion-conscious men are snapping them up, and *International Male* is now importing these shirts to America."

How do you like that? All those years, my grandmother would snap: "You look like a bum sitting on the steps in your underwear. Put a shirt on."

But he was simply a man ahead of his times.

The Greek undershirt isn't exactly like my grandfather's undershirt. His had buttons up the front and a higher neckline. And a few gravy stains, which he felt gave it character. But the general effect was the same.

Of course, my grandfather's undershirt was not imported from Greece. He was always loyal to Sears. As he used to say:

"If they had Sears stores in the old country that sold long underwear this good, most of us would've never left."

69

I pointed out the Greek undershirt ad to Sam Sianis, the Greek who runs Billy Goat's Tavern.

He said: "Shoo, dat's real Greek undershirt. I used to wear shirt like dees when I chase sheep. All men in my village wear shirt like dees."

Then he looked at the price, which was $22, and he shook his head.

He said: "No Greek pay $22 for undershirt. Maybe for a suit, but not no undershirt." Then he thought about it awhile. "Well, maybe Onassis. He might pay $22 for undershirt. But even Onassis, I bet for $22, he wants bottom, too."

It just shows the importance of timing. If my grandfather had been a young man in today's world, he would have been a fashion setter.

Simply by removing his shirt, he could have gone to the bars on Lincoln Avenue and looked right at home. True, he looked right at home on Milwaukee Avenue, too, but nobody accused him of being trendy.

Who knows, he might have even marketed his own designer long underwear.

But I'm not sure if they would have gone for the flap in the back.

The Coups That Changed Mankind

April 13, 1987

The world of science is delirious with excitement over the discovery of new, efficient ways to get electricity from here to there. Or there to here, I suppose.

It's said that these recent discoveries will have an enormous impact on the economy and our lifestyles and make possible all sorts of wondrous technological advances.

One scientist was quoted in this newspaper as saying about the rapid development and potential of the new electrical conductors: "Nothing like this has ever happened in science before."

Another said: "Superconductivity developments are the most exciting new breakthroughs of our lives. They will change the way we live."

With all respect for the scientists, I have my doubts about that. Changing the way we live, I mean.

For example, nothing I've read has said that this amazing breakthrough will lead to the elimination of some of the most terrible curses known to modern man— the rush-hour traffic jam, flavorless tomatoes, devious politicians or goofs who talk during the movies.

Every few years, scientists insist on telling us that something new and amazing will change our lives. But what happens? The military uses the new development to refine the methods we might use to blow up the world. And the rest of us wake up with the same problems, bills, aches and pains.

Consider the transistor, which replaced the vacuum tube and was hailed as one of the great inventions of the ages. What did it give us? A subrace of zombies who shuffle or jog through life with Walkman radios attached to their heads.

That's why I'm skeptical about most scientific breakthroughs. I've seen few of them lead to a genuine improvement in the way we live. Have any of them eliminated the hangover?

And that has led me to compile a list of what I consider to be some of the most important inventions of my lifetime. It isn't a comprehensive list, of course, and others may have their own choices. If so, you might send them to me and I'll add them to the list.

In no particular order, here are my choices.

● The automatic car wash, especially the kind that lets you shove a slug in a slot and squirt hot wax on your car. The automatic car wash has freed millions of men from the weekend ritual of slopping soap on their sneakers and has permitted them to do more important things, such as nothing.

● The disposable diaper. Only those who had children before it was available can appreciate how much less offensive it is to be a young parent. As Slats Grobnik once said: "Everybody says babies are so sweet. But if a grown man did the thing a kid does, he'd be run out of every saloon in town."

● The cut-proof golf ball. Scientists have estimated that this amazing advancement has eliminated so much stress that the average golfer's life has been extended by two and a half years. I made that up, but it's probably true anyway.

● The remote-control channel changer. The world would have been better off if TV had never been invented. What would we have missed—Sam Donaldson? But as long as we're stuck with it, it's nice to be able to flip through the channels effortlessly to see if there's anything lewd going on.

● The automatic ice cube maker. I can't imagine what life is like in societies that don't have this device. It's little wonder that there is so much discontent in the Third World.

● The one-size-fits-all men's stocking. Until we had this, we never knew whether a stocking would be too big or too little when we bought it. So most of us had toes that were either scrunched or pinched. As Plato said: A person cannot be truly happy with painful toes.

● 72

● The phone answering machine. It's been maligned and ridiculed. But it has permitted me to at last be honest with those who phone my home. Before I had one, I had to say "Hello. Oh, hi, how are you. Uh-huh, that's interesting. No kidding. Well, maybe we can get together and do that." Now, my recorded message states a simple truth: "I'm here, but I don't want to talk to you. At the beep, just go away. Thank you for listening."

As I said, others may have their favorites. Venetian blinds, for example, which admit light but discourage Peeping Toms; automatic windshield washers; and any garment made of polyester.

But we have a long way to go. We can put a man on the moon, and make electricity move more efficiently.

When will science develop a martini that is good for you?

Get the Picture?
Not at This Price

February 16, 1987

We were looking for something to fill blank space on the living room wall, which is how I found myself standing uncomfortably in an art gallery on a recent Saturday afternoon.

Art galleries are not my usual hangouts because—and I'm not embarrassed to admit it—I have little appreciation of visual art.

Some people are tone-deaf. To them, Beethoven's music sounds like a construction crew at work.

That's the way I am with paintings. My only reaction

73 ●

to the "Mona Lisa" is the thought that if she went into a singles bar, she'd spend the entire evening buying her own drinks. When I visited the Sistine Chapel, I looked at the ceiling and thought: "Boy, lying on that scaffold, I bet he got a stiff neck and a lot of paint in his eyes."

But, as I said, we have this empty space on the wall. And the female person who shares the living room said that we had to find something to hang there.

I suggested a calendar, the kind that has a different picture for every month. But she said that the smart set doesn't hang calendars on the living room wall.

She also rejected the suggestion that we put up a shelf and display my collection of old saloon-league softball trophies. She said they're not chic.

That's one of the things that confuses me about art. Recently, a famous artist made the cover of *Time* magazine when it was revealed that he had spent many years drawing his cleaning lady while she was naked. That is considered chic. But I ask—would you rather be known for persuading your cleaning lady to remove her skivvies or for hitting a home run to defeat Wally & Helen's Tavern?

Anyway, that's how I found myself in this art gallery, trying to blend in with the yuppies by cocking my head to one side, grasping my chin with my thumb and forefinger, peering at a painting and mumbling: "Hmmmm, interesting."

My act must have been convincing, because a woman who sold the paintings veered toward us and said: "Do you like that?"

"Yes," I said, and it was almost true. The painting appeared to be a long, thin, multicolored bird, and it wasn't bad. Actually, if a bird looking like that ever flew overhead, I'd probably dive under a porch. But at least I thought that I knew what it was, which is the first step in art appreciation.

Even more important, it seemed to be just the correct size to cover the blank space on the living room wall, which is the second step in art appreciation.

The gallery lady said: "And one of the nice things about this is that you can hang it this way or that way." And to demonstrate, she turned it so that it was hanging sideways. Then she turned it again, so it was upside down. Or maybe it was right side up.

"You see?" she asked.

That's why I'm embarrassed by my ignorance of art. If I decided to put a picture of my uncle Chester on the wall, I wouldn't think of hanging it upside down. In his prime, Uncle Chester wasn't much to look at, but the sight of him with his mouth above his eyes would turn a child's hair white.

Still faking it, I told the gallery lady: "Ah, very interesting. Either a diving or soaring effect, hey?"

Then she told me about the artist, a South American lady who now paints in New York and has been commissioned to do some posters. From her tone, I gathered that doing the posters was significant, although I don't know why. I've seen posters in Chicago that say "Elect Albert (Al) Zbygniewski Alderman, He Hates Crooks," and I wouldn't want them in my living room. Maybe the garage, though.

She also told how the South American lady worked. "She says she just gets up in the morning, throws the paint on the canvas and shifts it around until she gets the effect she wants."

My grandfather was a house painter, and if he had taken that approach, my grandmother would have wound up as a bag lady.

"It's reduced during our sale," the gallery lady said. Then she peered around the side of the frame, where they had stashed the price tag.

"It's reduced 40 percent," she said. "So you can have it for $4,800."

"Ahhh," I said. Or maybe it was more like "Huhhhh?"

The fact is, it wasn't a bad deal, considering that I could point a thing that might be a bird in any direction, up, down, north or south. In an earthquake, it would always look good.

But I told her that we would have to think about it and would drop back sometime.

We probably won't though. Next Saturday, I'm going to browse around some calendar stores.

Work the Bugs Out, Channel 11

March 26, 1985

A friend of mine asked if I had seen some wonderful television show recently presented on the public channel.

When I told him that I hardly ever watch that channel, he looked amazed.

"You don't watch public TV?" he said. "But that's the only station that shows anything of *quality.*"

That's what everybody always says. If you want to see thoughtful drama or fine music or shows with deep social significance, you are supposed to watch public TV.

Well, maybe they have such shows, but they're never there when I turn my set on.

No matter when I turn my set on, all I ever see is one of four shows:

1. Insects making love. Or maybe they are murdering each other. With insects, it's hard to tell the difference. But after a day's work, my idea of fun isn't watching a couple of bugs with six furry legs and one eye trying to give each other hickies.

● 76

2. A lion walking along with a dead antelope in its jaws. I don't know how many times I've seen that same mangy lion dragging that poor antelope into a bush. The tourist bureau in Africa must bring him out every time a TV crew shows up. But the question is, why do they keep showing it? Does somebody at the channel think that we must be taught that lions don't eat pizza?

3. Some spiffily dressed, elderly Englishman sitting in a tall-backed chair in a room that is paneled in dark wood. He is speaking to a younger Englishman who wears a World War I uniform and stands before a crackling fire. The older bloke says things like: "Well, Ralph, see you're back from the front. Jolly good luck that you weren't killed. Sorry to hear about your brother. Bloody bad luck, that. Shell took his head clean off. Oh, well, we must go on. Will you be joining us for dinner?" And the younger man says: "Thank you, Father."

4. The station announcer, talking about what great shows they have on Channel 11. The last time I tuned in, he talked about how great the next show was going to be. He talked about it for so long that I dozed off. When I awoke, he was talking about how great the show had been. Before I could get to the dial, two insects started making love again.

That's it. That's all I ever see on public TV.

Wait, I forgot. There are a couple of others.

Some skinny, bearded, squeaky-voiced, wimpy guy from Seattle does a cooking show. I have never seen a grown man get so excited about sautéing a Chinese pea pod. He even jiggles the pan so that the pea pod flips in the air. I guess he does that to prove he's macho.

And there's a show in which an intellectual carpenter clumps around somebody's old house, and they talk about refinishing the woodwork. The last time I happened to tune in, the intellectual carpenter and a yuppie couple were standing in the upstairs john and the young woman

77

was talking about improvements she was considering for her old toilet.

Now, let's say you've driven on the crowded expressways to and from your stress-filled job. You've finally made it home, had a couple of beers to calm your nerves, eaten dinner and you sit down to watch some TV.

And there is this woman pointing at her toilet bowl and saying "We are now working on the problem of the loud gurgle."

That's entertainment?

When I explained this to my cultured friend, he said, "What kind of *trash* do you prefer?"

The very best kind of trash, as a matter of fact. And I have found it on a show called *Lifestyles of the Rich and Famous.*

Recently, they had Lana Turner on, showing off her facelift and talking about how she was mysteriously drawn to visit Egypt because she is convinced that in another existence, many centuries ago, she lived there.

And I don't doubt her. Maybe in the good old days, Lana was a camel.

Regardless of what she was, it was better than hearing some Joan Baez lookalike talking about her gurgling toilet.

On another segment, the rich and famous were shown at a big party, wolfing down pounds of beluga caviar and quarts of $50 champagne. Sure, it was disgusting conspicuous consumption. But I'd rather watch that than that damn lion conspicuously consuming the dead antelope.

And if there is a starlet in a bikini who has been overlooked by the rich and famous cameras, she must be hiding.

"Ah, that's what you're interested in," sneered my cultured friend. "It's the T and A."

Well, it beats watching those insects going at it. With the starlets, I can tell which end is up.

Don't Blow Smoke—
Just Get Even

April 24, 1984

I rode a cab the other day that had a hand-drawn sign on the dashboard that said "No Smoking."

Although I smoke, complying with the sign wasn't a problem. I'm not the kind of smoker who makes a fuss about being deprived. If somebody doesn't want me to smoke in his presence, I don't. As nonsmokers everywhere are angrily saying, why should they be subjected to somebody else's smoke?

After we had gone about a block, I said, "Will you please turn off the noise?"

The cabdriver, a shaggy-haired man in his thirties, looked in his mirror and said, "The what?"

"The noise."

"You mean my radio?"

"Yes, the radio."

"What's wrong with it?" he said.

"It's giving me a headache. The music is bad and there's static. You ever hear of the problem of noise pollution? That's noise pollution."

He shook his head and turned it down.

"I can still hear it," I said.

"You want a different station? Some other kind of music?"

"No. I hate music. I haven't liked any music since Spike Jones' band."

79

He shook his head again but snapped the radio off. We rode in silence for less than a minute, when he said:

"You know, it's a funny thing about music. Some people, they like—"

I interrupted. "Say, no offense meant, but do you mind if we don't talk?"

"You don't want me to talk?" he said, sounding incredulous.

"Right."

"All right," he said, obviously offended. "Then I won't talk."

He probably thought I was rude or worse. Maybe you do, too. And maybe I sounded that way.

But just as he didn't want to be exposed to my smoke, why should I be exposed to his lousy taste in music, his radio's static and the sound of his voice?

Now, I have to admit that if the no-smoking sign hadn't been there, I might have felt differently. I would have opened the window a couple of inches so the smoke could escape, had a cigarette and listened to his music or his views on life.

But it's now my policy to meet intolerance with intolerance. I don't know if that's fair, but when it's over, I feel better.

It began awhile ago with one of two women at the next table in a restaurant. She was my first exposure to the antismoking crusaders.

I was having dinner with a pal. We hadn't even ordered when she turned toward me and said very firmly, "I'd appreciate it if you didn't smoke."

Before I could do anything but look surprised, she launched a California-style lecture. "Respecting rights of others . . . menace to the environment . . . intruding on my space. . . ."

Before she was finished, I had squashed my cigarette and said, "Okay, okay."

Because I'm a fair person, I could see her point. A little of my smoke might have drifted in her direction, although the place seemed well ventilated.

About halfway through the meal, I turned toward her and said, "Excuse me, but could I tell you something?"

"Yes?" she said, glaring at me in anticipation of the request she *knew* would come: Could I have just one cigarette?

But I fooled her. I didn't mention smoking at all. I just said: "I really don't care about your neighbor's medical problems. Or your job. Or your vacation plans. Would you lower your voices so your conversation doesn't intrude on my space?"

She knew exactly what I was up to. She gave me a look of contempt and said: "Really. The tables here are so close that we'd have to whisper."

"Try," I said. "I'd appreciate it."

But they didn't. She said, loudly and clearly: "Oh, he just thinks he's being *clever*. Oh, he's so"—and she dragged the word out—"so clevvvverrr." And they went on talking just as loudly.

That was it. War. I attacked on two fronts.

First, I told my friend a dirty joke. No, it wasn't dirty, it was filthy. It had no swearing or gutter language. But a really good, filthy joke is even filthier if told in clinical terms.

Then I told another. And their nostrils quivered and they ate faster.

It seemed only fair. If I had to hear about their neighbor's intestinal malfunctions, why shouldn't they hear my filthy jokes?

While I told the jokes, I took out my cigarettes and lighter and put them on the edge of the table.

When my last bite was gone, and the coffee cups filled, I picked up the cigarette package and sort of fondled it. I could see them watching.

Then I slowly slid out a cigarette and tapped it on the table. And tapped and tapped it. Then I put it between my lips. She was not only watching, she was starting to look homicidal.

I just kept it there for a minute. I took it out while I said something. Then I tapped it some more.

I picked up the lighter. But I just held lighter and cigarette in my hands, as if distracted by conversation.

Finally, I snapped the lighter a couple of times. She cracked under the pressure.

"Waiter," she said. "Check."

And they hadn't even had coffee or dessert.

As they rose, she glared at me and said, "Do you know what you are?"

I smiled, put down the unlit cigarette and said: "Thanks to you, much healthier."

So, you see, we can all coexist, if we just try.

Condo Man
Back Down to Earth

October 9, 1985

I suppose the tomato was a factor. I like tomatoes. But the kind sold in most stores taste like the plastic they're wrapped in. So I figured that if I wanted a good tomato, I'd have to grow my own. To do that, I'd need a backyard.

And that's why I am no longer Condo Man. About a week ago the moving truck came, and I have reverted to my natural state of Bungalow Man.

As I explained four years ago when I moved from a house on a side street into a lakefront condo, I was launching an anthropological study of those relatively new urban creatures, Condo Man, High-Rise Man, Lake-front Man, Health Club Man, Singles Bar Man and all the others.

To do this, I knew I couldn't watch from afar. I had to immerse myself in their native cultures, as social anthropologist Margaret Mead used to do. I had to become one of them.

Now the study is over, and I have to admit that it was a complete flop.

Oh, I tried. One of the first things I did was buy a genuine Bargongini 34-speed racing bike with a talitanium frame that weighed only 4½ ounces.

Slipping on my designer bike suit, I walked my bike into Lincoln Park, swung aboard and began pedaling along the lake. The bike creaked once or twice, then collapsed under me.

I carried the twisted wreckage into the bike shop and demanded a refund. The proprietor said: "We are not responsible. You are too heavy. It says right in the warranty: 'To be ridden only by the fashionably lean.' "

So I joined the New Vo Reesh Health Club and, in my velour running suit and my Nike shoes, set about creating a lean Lakefront Man body.

"This," the hulking instructor said as he patted the derricklike machine, "is the state of the art in exercise equipment. It will develop your quadrafeds, reduce your blats, strengthen your flipadids and do wonders for your claphs."

I strapped myself in and began lifting and pumping and kicking every which way. I found myself gasping and everything suddenly turned black.

When I came to, the instructor was standing over me with smelling salts, saying: "A close call. You caught your gold neck chain in the weight rack. Maybe you ought to try jogging."

So it was back to Lincoln Park, where I tried to learn

83

the ways of Jogging Man. And many of the experienced runners were generous in sharing their wisdom, such as the lean runner who said, "I don't want to intrude, but it really isn't good form to jog with a Pall Mall dangling from your lips."

Within a week I had increased my distance from ten yards to almost half a block. And I checked my pulse and found that, at the height of my workout, my rate went from its normal one hundred beats a minute to almost four hundred.

When I mentioned that to my doctor, he turned pale and said: "Why don't you just try walking? It's just as good for you, and it reduces the odds of your collapsing while running and the momentum carrying you into the lake."

So I took to taking brisk walks along Sheridan Road, Lake Shore Drive and Lake View Avenue.

But after only two days I displaced my hip socket and sprung a kneecap while leaping to avoid the sidewalk droppings of a pair of 200-pound Mastiffs. Their owner, a facelift under blue hair, said, "I'll thank you not to frighten my dogs."

During my recuperation, I decided to check out the scene at the singles bars. But I quickly left when a man appeared from behind a fern and said, "Looking for your runaway daughter?"

But it wasn't all bad. From my living room window I had a splendid view of the sun coming up over the lake. And over the Dopemobile, a camper that arrived in the park each morning to sell strange herbs and spices while a nearby policeman slipped tickets under windshield wipers.

And I fulfilled one goal: I found the elusive perfect pesto sauce for pasta.

When I told a neighbor of mine about my triumph, she waved her copy of *Chicago* magazine at me and said:

"You're so out of date. Nobody cares about pesto sauce any more. We're into Ethiopian cuisine. No silverware. You scoop up the yak stew with pieces of round bread."

So that was it for me. If I'm going to eat stews without silverware, I might as well do it somewhere in the direction of my old neighborhood.

And if somebody runs past my front door, I'll expect to see a cop chasing him.

Here's a Great Way to Tick Off Friends

December 17, 1986

Most of us have habits that can irritate our friends and loved ones.

With me, it's my wristwatch.

Ever since I discovered this make of watch several years ago, I've infuriated friends, coworkers and even casual acquaintances with conversations such as this:

"Nice watch you have there."

"Oh, thanks."

"One of those oyster-shell jobs, hmmm? Must be expensive."

"Gift from my wife."

"Beautiful. But tell me, what can it do?"

"Do? It tells the time."

At that point, I feign amazement and say: "That's all? For all that money, it only tells time?"

They usually fall into my trap by saying something like: "What do you expect a watch to do?"

I pull back my cuff, display my watch and show them.

While jabbing at the tiny buttons on its front and side, I say: "Besides keeping time in civilian or military mode, I expect it to be a fully functioning calculator. I also expect it to be an alarm clock. And to be a stopwatch. And to give me the day and date. And to beep on the hour."

In the past, I've had the model that not only did all those things but could play my choice of three popular tunes.

As well as light up in the dark.

But this year, I'm capable of being even more infuriating because I have the newest model, with the most amazing feature yet.

After I have run through the above tricks, I now say:

"By the way, let me have your unlisted phone number. I want to store it in my watch's data bank."

That really pops their eyes.

But it's true. Through the genius of Japanese technology, I can store fifty names and phone numbers in my watch.

I merely touch a button and the names and numbers scroll across the watch face.

And I usually conclude my performance by saying: "All that for $32.95 plus tax. Let's see, your watch cost about $500, right? Well, if I buy the latest, improved model of my watch every two years, at the end of thirty years . . ."

I pause to do some fast figuring in my watch's calculator mode, and say:

". . . At the end of thirty years, I'll have spent less for all of my amazing space-age, science fiction technology than you spent to, ha, ha, to find out what time it is."

It never fails to get a rise out of them. In fact, I have a friend who owns a $5,000 Rolex and no longer speaks to me.

That's because people like him feel foolish. They spend hundreds or even thousands of dollars, and for

● 86

what? To get information that is hanging on the walls of most homes and offices—the time of day.

But for only $32.95, I can tap a button and call up the unlisted number of my bookie. Or set the alarm to be sure that I don't oversleep at my desk and miss the cocktail hour.

I've never had as much satisfaction from a material possession.

That is, until I recently had a drink with an old friend I hadn't seen for a few years.

He was wearing one of those delicate, wafer-thin watches, made in France, I believe, so I couldn't resist going into my put-down routine.

"Must have cost a pretty penny," I said.

"A bundle," he said.

In a moment, I was putting my watch through its paces. But he just roared with laughter and said:

"I can't believe this. You? Wearing a nerd watch?"

"A what?"

"That's the kind of watches the nerds wear."

"Uh, you don't understand. This watch is also a calculator, a stopwatch, a phone directory, an alarm . . ."

He laughed again. "I know all that. That's why the nerds love them."

"Nerds? What do nerds have to do with it?"

"The computer nuts. The calculator freaks. The number crunchers. I've got a kid working in my office who has one exactly like it. Classic nerd. Keeps a slide rule, three pens, a tiny flashlight and a peanut butter sandwich in his shirt pocket."

"Uh, it's got a, uh, a two-year battery, you know?"

He slapped the bar and laughed uncontrollably. Then he said: "Who would have thought it? You, a nerd? Tell me, whatever possessed you to buy a watch like that?"

"Gift from my wife."

Broadway Joe
in Tobacco Road

September 23, 1985

While we were watching the last Bears game, Little George leaned away from the bar and said, "Hey, where is Joe Namath from?"

The bartender said: "He's from Pennsylvania. Town called Beaver Falls."

"That's what I thought. Then why does Namath talk that way?"

"What way?"

"He talks like a Southerner. Or a black guy. Listen."

So we listened to Namath's commentary. And he was right. It was a "lawn pass" for long pass. It was "laif" for left, "plez" for plays, "plehr" for player, "bah" for by, "tron" for trying, "lahn-min" for linemen and "suh-prahzed" for surprised.

"That's very strange," Little George said. "I've been in that part of Pennsylvania. And people don't talk that way. They talk like we do, like Midwesterners."

"Well," the bartender said, "he played college ball in Alabama. Maybe he picked it up there."

"That was twenty years ago. And he spent a lot more time than that in New York, but he doesn't talk like a New Yorker."

"Then why does he talk like a Southerner?"

I interrupted to explain this phenomenon.

What they were hearing is a dialect that has crept into American speech. I call it Yuppabilly because it is often spoken by white Northern yuppies who, for whatever reason, want to sound like Southerners or blacks.

I first noticed the Yuppabilly dialect when I heard a former yuppie coworker of mine speaking it. If you didn't

88

know him, you would have thought he was from Arkansas or some such rustic place.

In fact, he was from a wealthy New England suburb and had attended Ivy League schools.

But he developed his Yuppabilly dialect because he was single and discovered that he could impress more females in singles bars if he spoke with a drawl. It provided him with a more rakish, macho, good-old-boy personality than did his Yale background.

Actually, Yuppabilly has some of its roots in the folk music revival of the late 1950s and early '60s, when white suburban youths began plunking guitars and banjos and singing songs about "Ah bin swingin' a six-poun' hammer fum mah hips on down." Bob Dylan, the son of a Jewish hardware store owner in Minnesota, became a star when he learned to sing and talk like a 1930s Dust Bowl Okie.

And that spilled over into rock music. One reason nobody can understand rock lyrics, besides the deafening decibels, is that everybody is singing in some sort of Southern or black drawl. You even hear English rockers howling "C'mawnn all you pee-puhhlll, let's git togayder."

The urban cowboy fad helped the spread of Yuppabilly, with MBAs wearing $150 boots going in singles bars and saying "Mah pu-laise or yores?"

The CB craze contributed, too. Everybody who talked into a CB tried to sound like a corn-pone trucker.

To confirm my theory on Namath, I called a few people in his hometown and asked about how they talked and how he used to talk.

[I interrupt to point out that his name isn't really Joe Willie. It is Joseph William. Few parents of Hungarian ancestry give their kids names like Joe Willie. Or Bubba. Or Billy Bob.]

An editor at the Beaver Falls newspaper said: "No, we don't talk that way. We sound like other Midwesterners." And a writer who knew Namath when he was a kid said,

"He used to talk like all of the other kids."

For an expert's view, I asked Ellen Schauber, an associate professor of linguistics at Northwestern University, whether some people develop accents to be trendy.

"Absolutely," she said, "some accents become trendier than others. Every accent brings a characterization of one's self or one's society. Through an accent, they associate themselves with groups."

Maybe that explains Namath's accent. He spent many years playing college and professional football. And part of his job as a quarterback involved being chased and fallen upon by gigantic linemen, most of whom seem to be either black or white Southerners.

Maybe Namath thought that if he talked like them, they wouldn't fall on him as hard.

To Tell the Truth,
He's a Real Loser

September 4, 1984

When the winning lottery numbers were announced on TV, there was moaning and swearing up and down the bar. But Herbert took it calmly. He shrugged and said, "Unlike these fools, I was absolutely certain I wasn't going to win."

But how could you be sure? Anybody with a ticket has a chance.

"No, that isn't true. I don't know how it's done, but somehow things are rigged so that certain people can't win. People like me."

What do you mean, people like you?

"We have certain characteristics."

Such as?

"Well, let's start with Hawaii. I don't like Hawaii. I would never consider going there."

So?

"So this. About half the people who win a big lottery say the same thing: They're going to use some of their winnings for a vacation in Hawaii. Never Paris or a villa near Rome. Never Martha's Vineyard or Palm Springs. It's always Hawaii. Why do people who suddenly get rich want to fly thousands of miles to eat a pig cooked in a hole in the ground?"

An interesting question.

"Yes, and another reason I don't qualify is that I don't have a sister in California."

What does that have to do with it?

"The ones who don't go to Hawaii usually say they are going to use their winnings to visit their sister in California. How's that for life in the fast track?"

I suppose it could be livelier.

"Yes, and I'm not going to buy any new furniture or a new TV set or add a rec room to my house, which winners always say they're going to do. I would announce that I was going to burn down the dump and every dull object in it."

Your wife wouldn't like that.

"That's probably true. So I also would announce that I was going to retain the best divorce lawyer in America to rid me of her."

That's rather callous of you, considering all those years she's given you.

"Actually, it's generous of me. It's not like I was going to hire someone to bump her off, which I could well afford to do if I won the lottery. Now that would be callous. And I wouldn't do it unless she was unreasonable."

But what would your friends think?

"As friends, I hope they would understand. I would

write them letters, explaining everything and telling them how I was going to save our friendship."

How would you do that?

"By having nothing further to do with any of them."

That's not very friendly.

"Of course it is. Human nature being what it is, if I won they would all become terribly envious. This would cause friction in our friendship. So to save them from this painful situation, I would tell them that I didn't want to see them again. And if they showed up, I'd have my body-guards throw them out."

But wouldn't you share some of your new wealth with them?

"That would be a terrible thing to do to my friends. It would make them dependent upon me, which would be wrong because they would never know if they would have succeeded in life on their own. Naturally, they'll fail on their own. But at least through failure they will come to know themselves. That precious self-knowledge would be my true gift of friendship to them."

But how can somebody live without friends and loved ones?

"Oh, that's no problem. I would simply go to the French Riviera and put up a sign on my yacht saying: 'I have $40 million. Do you love me?' Believe me, the world is filled with loving people. They would probably love me so much they would be willing to do light housekeeping and my laundry, too."

But you can't just spend your life as a playboy.

"Why not? Why can't there be just one lottery winner who looks into the TV cameras and says: 'I am going to quit my job, dump my wife, shed my friends and use my wealth to do all the unspeakable things most of you dream about but are ashamed to admit.'"

Because that would discredit the lottery. It isn't intended to shatter marriages and turn decent men into sinful idlers.

"You might be right. So if I ever win, I'll revise my plan. I'll stay with my wife."

That's the way.

"Yes. And I'll get six mistresses."

Time to Tell Off Jerks
Who Tell All

September 30, 1985

There's a train that goes through the mountains of Utah on the way to the Pacific Coast. A few hundred feet up one of the mountains is the mouth of a small cave where a hermit lives.

A conductor who has ridden the route for years, and seems to know every foot of the way, once pointed it out to me. "I don't know what his name is, but I hear that he used to live in a city and had a successful job. Then he packed it in a few years ago, and now that's where he lives. He's supposed to have it fixed up pretty nice. He comes into town once in a while. I've seen him come out of the cave when the train goes by. He doesn't wave or anything. He just stands there and watches."

Somebody I was traveling with offered a suggestion. "On the trip back, why don't you get off the train at the next stop? You could rent a car, drive here and get up there and interview him. It might make a fascinating story. There can't be too many genuine hermits."

I thought about it, then decided it was a bad idea. Not that it wouldn't make an interesting story, if the conductor

93 ●

was accurate and if the hermit was willing to talk about why he wanted to live alone in a remote cave.

But what would the result of the story have been? After me, there would be the TV cameras. Maybe *60 Minutes* would be trudging up the side of the hill to demand to know why the man preferred a cave over a condo. And that might lead to offers of book contracts.

Then the poor guy would wind up in *People* magazine, and who knows what that would lead to? A showbiz career? Doing beer commercials?

No, there aren't enough people who want to avoid being seen or listened to, and we shouldn't disturb those who do. What we need are more hermits and fewer celebrities; more people who say "no comment" instead of "I have called this press conference to announce plans for my . . ."

Unfortunately, we're in the age of full disclosure, with celebrities blabbing about every detail of their lives to anyone who will listen. Among the full-disclosure trends have been:

● Love-child chic. When an actress becomes pregnant by her costar or director, can't she just go off for a few months to stay with relatives? Does she have to pose for tummy pictures and announce that she and the prospective daddy are thinking of getting engaged?

● Drying-out chic. This has become intensely competitive. Actress A says she has been drinking a fifth of gin or a bottle of wine a day and is going to enter a California sanitarium to get rid of the shakes. Not to be outdone, Actress B says she's been drinking a fifth of vodka a day, plus swallowing a jar of tranquilizers, and is entering the same sanitarium to get her eyes uncrossed. Then Actor C says that he has been drinking a fifth a day *plus* taking tranquilizers and using grass and uppers, and he is going to take the cure and begin jogging. Then Ballplayer D says that he is sniffing a kilo a day and is going into a sanitarium so he can come down from the ceiling. Why can't they just stay in bed on a Sunday morning and quietly moan like everybody else?

● Memoirs chic. This is probably the worst, with aging stars writing about every person with whom they shared a bed or couch. Or the offspring of stars writing about how nasty Mommy or Daddy was to them. Reading these books can make you wish that Mommy and Daddy had been mean enough to toss the brats out the window.

Of course, the reason everybody blabs is that there is a market for it. We've become a nation of Peeping Toms.

Consider the top nonfiction best-seller on the current book lists. It's a book by Elvis Presley's ex-wife about her life with the singer, and it's selling by the hundreds of thousands and will soon go into the millions.

The question is, why? By now everybody knows that Presley doped himself to death, that he led an eccentric, self-indulgent life.

The book is selling because the former Mrs. Presley tells about their sex life and about a couple of her own affairs, and people who have not read a book since Dick and Jane are eager to look through the Presley transom.

Now, I can understand a person needing to share these intimate details. Maybe with an understanding friend over a few drinks.

But with millions of strangers? I mean, would you turn to the person standing next to you on the bus and say: "Shall I tell you how me and my husband do it?"

Enough. I don't want to know any more about the sleeping arrangements of the rich and famous, or who is coming out of the closet, or who is carrying whozit's baby, or who is coming off a three-year bender.

What we need are more hermits. Of course, maybe that's why the guy in Utah became a hermit in the first place. He couldn't stand listening to any more of it either.

Padded Cell 3

"Double-lock the Doors!"

I've Fully Paid
My Victim Tax

June 28, 1984

The detective put two photo albums on my desk and said: "If he's in there, you might recognize him."

The albums were huge. They were filled with front and side pictures of thugs, stick-up men, muggers, pimps, purse snatchers and all-around thieves.

Halfway through, I said: "You must have every bum in Chicago in here."

The cop shook his head. "No. Those are just the ones from your area."

It was an awesome thought: all those mean, moronic mugs plying their trade in my neighborhood alone. And if you add together all the mugs in the other neighborhoods, they're the size of an army. In fact, there are probably many nations whose armies aren't as big as Chicago's street mug population. Or as mean. Or as well armed.

In a way it made me feel better about having been robbed. If there were that many of them out there, being robbed seemed almost natural. Not being robbed was unnatural.

As a friend of mine put it: "It's sort of like a tax we pay for living in the city. A victim tax."

If so, I'm a solid taxpayer. Looking back, my victim tax adds up like this:

Robbery: This is my second one. The first time was about fifteen years ago, when I was covering a story on the South Side and a group of large punks took my money and watch. They didn't have guns, though. They relied on muscle.

I also had a near-miss a few years ago. They came out of a dark gangway, but because they were wearing those goofy high-heeled shoes, I outran them.

Burglaries: Three. The last time was when they battered down the door of my old house. Eventually they were caught and turned out to be kids from prosperous suburban families. When he learned that his son was a burglar, the father of one of them pitched over with a massive heart attack. The judge sentenced them to see a shrink.

Car theft: Three. Once they went joy riding, then dumped the car in front of an alderman's house. I don't know if that was a coincidence or they had a sense of humor. The next time they stripped it and left it in a forest preserve. The last time it vanished forever, probably in a chop shop.

Actually, I'm getting a little tired of it. My neck is stiff from looking over my shoulder. While city life has its charms, I don't like having to guess whether the guy walking toward me on the dark side street has a shiv up his sleeve. He probably doesn't like the feeling either.

It's not the money. The two punks in my building's outer lobby got about $95. My stolen cars were insured. So was the stuff taken in my house burglaries.

But I don't like looking down the barrel of a gun. Especially when the guy holding it is nervously hopping from one foot to another, twitching, breathing hard, and I'm wondering if the stupid bastard is going to blow me away.

It's also the indignity of it all. I'm a grown man. I've fought in a war, married, raised my kids, buried my dead, paid my bills, worked hard at my job and never mooched a dollar from anyone.

And there I was, wondering if it was all going to end on an impulse by an illiterate punk with the IQ of a turnip. It lasted less than a minute, but it isn't a pleasant feeling to know that your life is in some punk's grubby hands.

But what do you do? An hour after I was robbed, I was depressed because I realized I wasn't my father's son.

It happened to the old man many years ago. He was a milkman. One morning, before dawn, a guy with a knife started to climb into his truck. The old man kicked him in the face. The guy got up and ran. The old man slammed his truck into gear, drove on the sidewalk, floored the gas pedal and—bump, bump—the world had one less stick-up man.

I could have done the same. My car was at the curb, only a few feet away. I could see them running down my street. In a few seconds, I could have caught them. I'm sure the insurance would have covered any damage to my bumper.

But it didn't even cross my mind. In my father's day, people fought back with ferocity. In my day, we pay the victim tax and wonder what sociological forces brought the poor lad to a life of crime.

All things considered, running them over is a much better idea.

Of course, his mother would probably sue me. And collect. So I guess I got off cheap.

Me with a Gun?
Control Yourself

July 2, 1984

There was a surge of triumph in his voice.

"After what happened to you," he said, "maybe now you'll feel a little different about gun control."

I told him that I honestly didn't understand what he was talking about.

"What I mean is that maybe now you'll see how we gun owners feel when people talk about taking away our guns."

I told him that I still didn't understand what he was talking about.

"Well, if you had a gun . . ."

If I had a gun?

"Sure, if you had a gun, you could have defended yourself. And that's all most of us are interested in— defending ourselves."

Now I understood him. When I was robbed last week, I was not armed. But if I had been armed, I could have avoided being robbed. I might have even captured the robber. Right?

"Well, yes."

That's a dramatic scenario, so let's expand it. I'm in the vestibule of my building. A man with a gun bursts in. His partner waits outside as a lookout. The man puts the gun to my face, in the general area of my nose, which is quite a general area.

Now, let's assume that I own a pistol. Chances are that I wouldn't have it in my pocket or waistband, since it's illegal to carry a concealed weapon.

More likely it would be upstairs in my apartment, probably in a drawer next to the bed, which is where most gun owners stash their guns. (That makes it more convenient for them to wake in a fright and shoot their wives, children, dogs or feet. Far more family members and feet are shot in this country's bedrooms than burglars and fiends.)

Obviously, I have a problem. He is pointing a gun at my nose. But my gun is upstairs in a nightstand drawer. So what do I do?

I suppose I could call upon his sense of sportsmanship and say: "Would you mind waiting a moment while I go upstairs and get my gun, and we can settle this man to man?"

He didn't seem the sporting type.

Or I might have been devious and said: "Here's my money. Boy, am I lucky. This is just chickenfeed. I've got more than $50,000 stashed away in a drawer in my bedroom. I'm sure glad it's up there and not in my pocket."

This would arouse his greed, we'd go to my apartment, I would reach into the drawer, whip out my pistol and drop the gullible fellow with a fast shot.

I don't think he'd fall for it. And if he did, he might want to check the nightstand drawer himself. Wow, would he be mad at me.

No, what I would have done if I owned a gun that was upstairs is exactly what I did anyway. I would have given him my money and felt enormously relieved when he departed.

But for the sake of argument, let's say that I owned a gun and had it on me.

103 ●

That's possible. While it's illegal, many Chicagoans carry pistols in their pockets or purses, and the vast majority are never caught unless they shoot somebody or get drunk and flaunt the weapon in a bar.

So I could be carrying a gun. And let's resume the scenario. I'm in my vestibule, my door keys in my hand. The man bursts in, I turn and I see the gun near my nose.

Do I reach for my gun at the moment? Of course not. He has only to move his finger an inch or less, and I get a bullet in the nostril.

I wait for him to tell me to give him my money. When he does, I reach into my pocket and—surprise!—I pull out a gun instead.

Unfortunately, he watches my hand going into my pocket. And if it emerges with a gun instead of a wallet, things might get sticky. He might squeeze his trigger before I squeeze mine. In which case, I lose.

Or he might hesitate long enough for me to squeeze the trigger at the same time he squeezes the trigger. I earn a draw, which wouldn't be bad in a chess game, but not in a shootout.

Or maybe he is a big phony and is really timid and afraid of guns. And when he sees mine, he begs for mercy. It's possible. But someone who makes his living by prowling the streets at night with a large automatic in his hand might be many things: mean, stupid, even rude to his mother. But I doubt if he's timid.

So I wouldn't do it, unless I was feeling suicidal. Even with a gun in my pocket, I'd still give him the money.

Then, I suppose, I could wait until he backed out of the vestibule and started running. I could draw my gun, dash outside, aim and try to bring him down.

If I was a good shot, I might do it. Or I might miss, and he might turn and shoot at me. Who knows what the outcome would be?

But the odds are outlandish. First, I'd have to own a gun and it would have to be in my pocket. I'd have to shoot a moving target twenty to thirty feet away.

My question to gun advocates is this: Why doesn't it happen more often? With all the guns in this country, why are stick-up men and other criminals so seldom shot?

As that caller said: "I don't know. But I've got a gun and I feel better having it."

Yeah, but where were you and your gun when I needed you?

Squeeze Out No Tears
for Tony

June 24, 1986

One evening, I spotted Tony Spilotro sitting a couple of tables away in a Rush Street restaurant. He was eating linguine with white clam sauce, which is what I had ordered.

When I told the people I was with who he was, one of them said: "Why don't you go over and talk to him? It might make a story."

I shook my head. "He makes me nervous."

He said: "Why? You've talked to other people in the mob."

That was true. As part of my job, I've interviewed mugs like Joey Glimco, when he was the big heat of the Chicago Teamsters.

When Joey said he really wasn't a gangster, I asked him why everybody said he was.

105 ●

He shook his head and said: "It was all them Irish cops that did it. They were always arresting me for nothing when I was a young guy."

Why did they pick on you?

"I guess they didn't like Italians," he said.

And I once convinced Sam DeStefano that he'd make a terrific movie critic. My idea was to take him to see *The Godfather* when it first came out, so I could sit next to him and tape his observations for my column. I assured him that the nation's moviegoers would be fascinated by his expertise.

Sam, who had a big ego, agreed to do it if the Chicago Theatre would block off the first five rows for his bodyguards.

It was all set up, but at the last minute the deal fell through when Tony Accardo, Chicago's mob boss, sent word that Sam should keep his fat mouth shut.

Later, somebody shut Sam's mouth for good.

Then there was my neighbor and regular pinochle partner, Richard Cain, a well-known cop who unfortunately had expensive tastes. He went bad, did a stretch in prison and went to work for Sam Giancana.

The last time I saw him, he and Giancana had just returned from exile in Mexico. He told me he had big plans, very, very big.

He didn't elaborate, but apparently somebody didn't like his big plans and sent around a couple of guys with ski masks and shotguns. End of big plans.

There were others. Big Angie, a former schoolmate, became a button man for Willie "Potatoes" Daddano. But when Angelo became a stoolie for the FBI, somebody stooled on him. I guess you just can't trust anybody. The embalmer had a heck of a time filling Angie's ice pick holes.

Considering all that, why would Tony Spilotro make me nervous?

As I explained to my friends that night: "Spilotro once put somebody's head in a vise."

"A vise?"

"Yes, the kind of vise you'd find in a basement tool shop."

"Why did he do that?" they asked.

The answer was that Spilotro wanted the man to give him some information. The man didn't want to give him the information, so Spilotro put his head in the vise and tightened it.

They didn't say anything for a few moments.

Then one of them asked: "What happened?"

What happened was that when the vise got tight enough, and the guy's skull starting making creaking sounds, he told Spilotro what he wanted to know.

Then Spilotro cut his throat from ear to ear.

So that was why I didn't try to talk to Tony Spilotro. While it's true that just about anybody connected with organized crime is capable of being nasty, there's something unusually nasty about someone who will squeeze another human being's head in a vise.

For the rest of the meal, my friends just picked at their food.

And one of them said something like: "It's hard to believe. Sitting there, eating with his friend, he looks just like anybody else. Just an ordinary guy."

That depends on whether you're looking at him in a restaurant or from the tight end of a vise.

But now Tony's head-squeezing days are over. His second-to-last resting place was a cornfield in Indiana, where he and his brother were dumped for reasons we'll probably never know.

Thinking back to that restaurant, though, there is one question I would like to have asked.

Didn't anybody ever tell him that you don't put Parmesan on white clam sauce?

107 ●

Were They Cruising
for a Shooting?

August 10, 1987

There's something very strange about the outbreak of shootings on California's freeways.

If you read the accounts of the shootings, you probably notice that just about all of the victims say essentially the same thing about their own behavior.

They were just cruising along, minding their own business, not bothering anyone and scrupulously observing the rules of the road.

Then suddenly, almost out of nowhere, some madman in another car began shooting at them.

I suppose it's possible that this is true, that people who carry guns in their cars have suddenly developed a mass hatred of courteous, inoffensive drivers.

But I would find it all a bit more realistic if some of those whose cars were punctured said something like this:

"I'm driving home from work, see. Hate my job, the boss picks on me, nobody there gives me any respect. When I get home, me and the wife will have another argument, and she'll win like she always does. That's why I like being in my car. Nobody messes with me in my car.

"Anyway, I see this guy coming down the ramp to get on the freeway. He's speeding up to merge in my lane. He's going to try to pull in ahead of me. Hey, nobody gets ahead of me. I don't have to take that kind of abuse. So I speed up. He speeds up. But I ain't letting this turkey get one up on me.

"So I stomp the pedal. Now he's running out of room. Hah, I almost run the sucker right up on the grass. But at the last second he chickens out and slams on the brakes. I showed him a thing or two.

"The next thing I know, he pulls up next to me and he's yelling something. I just give him the finger like I wish I could do to my boss. Then—I can't believe it—this guy whips out a gun and puts a bullet through my window. He tries to kill me! I'll tell you, there are some crazy people out there."

Or maybe this:

"So I'm hauling this big load from Portland down to San Diego and I've been on the road all day. I'm mad because when I went to shake a couple of uppers out of the bottle, they spilled all over the floor and I don't have time to stop. In my business, time is money.

"Anyway, I'm moving good when I hit this mess of traffic. Cars. Little cars. I hate them. Sometimes I have dreams where they're all over me, crawling up my legs, biting me. And I have fantasies where I'm doing ninety in a giant steamroller and I flatten them like bugs.

"Like I say, I hit this traffic and there's this little car in front of me, one of those expensive sports jobs. And if I could get by him, I could save maybe fifteen seconds on my run. But he's in my way. What's he doing out there anyway? I mean, I'm making a living. He's just getting in my way. Guys like that ain't fit to live. Fancy car. Lots of money. And nothing better to do than make me miserable.

"So I figure I'll teach him a lesson. I get closer. I get back on his tail and stay there. Then I drop back a little and come barreling up and stay on his butt. The rich little twit. His father probably bought him the car.

"Then you know what he does? He taps his brakes, like he's going to warn me. Oh, the punk. So I get even closer. I got him boxed in. He can't go nowhere, and I know he's looking in that mirror and he sees me and he knows that if he screws up just a little, I'm going to turn him into a blob.

"I stay there for two, three miles. Finally there's an opening in the next lane and the dirty little coward swerves to get out of my way. So I barrel past him and the next thing I know, I hear pop, pop, pop. The nut is shooting holes in my door.

"I'll tell you, Officer, it ain't safe out here for professional drivers anymore."

Or possibly this:

"I'm riding along in the fast lane, talking to my buddy. We're just cruising around, see. Then I notice this jerk in a van behind me. Some kind of delivery guy. And the way he's coming up on me, it's like he owns the whole road.

"So I figure, 'Hey, you want to go faster, go around.' Of course, he can't get around because of the traffic. That's his tough cookie.

"I can tell he's getting mad. Too bad. If he wasn't a jerk, he wouldn't be running deliveries.

"So he finally gets in the other lane and starts to pass. So I figure, 'Okay, wise guy. I want to see how fast you can go,' and I hit the gas and stay right with him.

"Then you know what he does, he cuts in front of me. I mean, he almost takes off my bumper. So I tell my buddy I'm going to show him who he's messing with. And I hit the gas hard and I wheel around and I cut him off. Then I stomp my brakes. I mean, does he think I'm some chump?

"So he switches lanes to pass me again, but I'm too quick for him. I swing out and block him. Then he goes around the other side, but I get in front. I mean, you got to teach jerks a lesson, right?

"Then he slows down and falls back. I figure he learned his lesson. All of a sudden, he floors it and comes up like a maniac. I look at him and, my God, he's pointing something at me. He's blowing his horn and aiming this thing at me. I got so scared, I swerved off the road and almost rolled over. My heart was pounding.

"Hey, what's the world coming to with all these wackos out there?"

Now, I'm not saying that those who are being menaced might sometimes bring it on themselves. It's entirely possible that there's something about courteous, sensible drivers that brings out the homicidal beast in some people.

If so, how can the guys with the guns find such a tiny minority?

He'd Cut Off Nose
to Spite His Fate

October 31, 1986

I suppose that under our laws, Judge Prentice Marshall's ruling was correct. But he sure passed up an intriguing deal.

I'm referring to the compromise that was offered to Judge Marshall by a convicted drug smuggler a few days ago.

The drug dealer, a native of Pakistan named Haji Yameen, had been found guilty of bringing a big load of heroin into this country.

When the moment came for him to be sentenced, Yameen, who is in his thirties, was given an opportunity to speak in his own behalf.

Yameen said he realized he would have to be punished, even though the jury had made a terrible mistake and he was really innocent.

But since he had been found guilty, did the punishment have to be prison? No, Yameen said, it didn't.

Yameen said that back in Pakistan, he has a wife and children whom he loves dearly. If he was locked up in an American prison, he would not see his family for many years. Even worse, he could not provide for them and in that impoverished country, they might have difficulty surviving.

So he offered the judge a deal.

"Instead of sending me to prison," he said, "cut off my nose."

Every jaw in the courtroom dropped. "It really freaked me out," said the federal prosecutor, Howard Pearl.

"My ears, too," he said. "And a hand. And a foot. Cut them all off. That would be punishment and I could go home to my family."

Judge Marshall, who never before had been offered a defendant's nose, much less any ears, hands or feet, explained that in this country we don't lop off noses or any other appendages.

Yameen looked disappointed. But he quickly offered another proposal.

If he had to go to prison, would the judge please allow his wife and children to come here from Pakistan and join him in his cell?

In other words, lock the family up with him. It might get a little cramped, but at least they'd be together.

Once again, the judge had to explain. We don't permit the families of convicted criminals to set up housekeeping in prison cells. Yameen would have to serve his sentence by himself.

And he sentenced Yameen to six years in a federal prison.

As I said, the judge was undoubtedly correct. Under our system of law, the removal of a nose would be considered cruel and unusual punishment. Instead, we send people to prisons where their fellow inmates can cut off their noses.

But it makes me wonder if we ought to think about Yameen's offer and some of the possibilities it presents.

As everybody knows, our prisons are so overcrowded that we have to let criminals out early just to make room for a new batch of fiends.

So, maybe we should provide judges and convicted criminals, such as Yameen, with options.

For example, when Yameen said, "Cut off my nose," the judge could have said, "Okay, I'll lop off three years if we lop off your nose."

After all, it is Yameen's nose. And if he can do without it, who are we to argue?

Then Yameen could have said: "That leaves me with three more years. How much are my ears worth?"

The judge could have said, "I'll knock off a year for each ear."

"That leaves one year," Yameen might have said. "How about two big toes and we'll call it even?"

"You got a deal," the judge might have said.

That way Yameen could have returned to his family. If they really love him, they'd overlook his altered appearance. Besides, he could always go to a novelty shop and buy one of those plastic party noses that are held on by a piece of elastic.

And we would save the thousands of tax dollars that we'll now spend to keep Yameen in a cell.

This could be a solution to the cell shortage, and it also could be a way of reducing crime. Especially sex crimes, if the offenders would agree to the removal of the appropriate appendage.

And there may be some precedent for this type of arrangement. At least there is in Chicago.

As we all know, some Chicago judges have turned

criminals loose after being given something of value by the defendants or their lawyers.

The only difference I can see is that the judge might have a hard time depositing a nose in his secret bank account.

Oh, Pops,
You Done Us Proud

February 13, 1985

The cops grabbed "Pops" Panczko the other day. The silly old geezer was messing around with a jewelry salesman's car. Imagine that—at sixty-six, he's still out there on a cold day stealing. It just shows what pride can do.

That's right, I said pride. Some people probably assume that Pops, who was once Chicago's best-known thief, steals simply for profit.

Well, that's part of it, of course. Everything Pops has stolen in his long career was worth *something*. The man is, after all, a professional.

But there's been more to it. There was his pride as a steady workman. Since he was a young man growing up near Humboldt Park in the Depression, he has believed in getting up every day, washing his face, shaving and going out into the city to steal something.

On slow days, it might have been only a crate of onions. On better days, it might be a rack of fur coats or a tray of diamond rings.

You don't get yourself pinched more than a thousand times, by Pops' own estimate, if you are finicky. Nor do you earn enough money to pay lawyers to keep you out on the street working.

And there was pride that went beyond that of the working thief. It was a pride that kept him from going legit when he had the chance.

Yes, Pops once had a chance to become a celebrity, a literary figure, a darling of talk shows. He could have made *Donahue*. But he rejected it.

The chance came about twelve years ago, and this is the story.

I was having a beer with a visiting book editor from New York. He happened to have read a newspaper story about Pops being arrested for stealing a truckload of lawn mowers or something like that. And he asked me about it.

"Oh, that's not unusual," I told him. "Pops' brother Butch was once grabbed for stealing a cement mixer out in the suburbs. He was driving it back to Humboldt Park on the expressway."

"Did he go to prison?" the book editor asked.

"No, he beat the rap, but I think they got him for driving the cement mixer while under the influence."

"Do they always do things like that?"

"Well, Peanuts, another brother, once did a jewelry heist in Florida and tried to escape by speedboat. But his gang forgot to untie the lines, and they never left the pier."

The New York editor was intrigued. So I told him about the time Pops was caught inside a jewelry store at about two in the morning. He told the jury that he had a need to go to the bathroom, and the door of the store was open. The jury was impressed that Pops was too gentlemanly to relieve himself on the street, so they set him free.

Then there was the slugs caper. Pops found that he could use slugs in almost any vending machine. And many of them would give change. But the FBI got him for also using slugs to make long distance calls, and he stood trial.

In a recess in the trial, his lawyer had to phone his office. "You got any change?" he asked Pops. "No," Pops said, offering him a handful of slugs. "But these'll work."

"My goodness," the New York editor said, "the man sounds like a complete incompetent."

"Well, I guess he is in a way. All the Panczkos were. They would plan great heists, then they'd tell everybody in the saloon about them, and somebody would stool to the cops and they'd usually be waiting."

"Do you know Pops?"

"Sure. For years. We came from the same neighborhood."

And so the editor offered the deal. A book contract for Pops' life story. He said it would be a cinch for a movie sale. And maybe a TV spinoff. Pops would make a fortune.

A few days later, I was in the office of Pops' lawyer. He almost salivated when I told him how much the New York publisher was willing to advance Pops.

"It would take him five years to steal that much," the lawyer said.

I told him that was just for the hardcover book. The paperback rights, the movie deal and the TV deal would bring in much more.

"My God," the lawyer said. "Pops can finally pay me."

When Pops came in, carrying an armload of briefcases he had just lifted from the delivery truck downstairs, I told him about the offer.

"All I have to do is talk to you about my work?" he said.

"That's all. We'll use a tape recorder, and I'll do the rest."

"And I'll get rich?" Pops asked.

"You'll wow 'em in New York and Hollywood."

"I'll do it," Pops said.

We shook on the deal. And Pops pulled up his coat

sleeve, showing an arm with a dozen watches and said: "Here, take one."

But a week later we met, and he said: "I can't do it."

"Why not?"

"My sister doesn't want me to. And I think she's right."

"What did she say?"

"She said it would embarrass the family. It would ruin the name."

So, that's why Pop is still out there, eyeing a salesman's car or a crate of onions.

And the next time you read some movie star's shameless book about her 6 marriages and 138 affairs, think of Pops and his pride.

But remember to lock your car.

State's Philosophy Can't Cut Mustard

March 26, 1987

An official-looking piece of mail arrived at Erik's Deli in Oak Park the other day.

Matt Mueller, the manager, opened the envelope and found some forms that the state wanted him to fill out.

They concerned a young man named Anthony, who used to be a busboy at the deli. Anthony was out of work and wanted the state to give him unemployment compensation.

Mueller sat down and remembered what he knew about Anthony.

In the beginning, Anthony had been a reasonably

competent busboy. He filled the water glasses, cleaned off the tables and washed his hands when he went to the bathroom.

But after a few weeks, he seemed to lose his enthusiasm and energy. He'd show up late for work, leave tables half cleared, and his mind seemed to be somewhere else.

Mueller would tell him, "Anthony, you have to work harder." Anthony would shrug and say he was doing his best.

After about three or four such conversations, Mueller told Anthony that he was through. Anthony shrugged. Being fired didn't seem to bother him.

A few days later, something strange happened at the deli.

One of the night-shift employees was taking out a can of garbage. When he opened the door, he met three men wearing masks and surgical gloves. One of them had a gun.

They grabbed him and dragged him inside. They quickly rounded up the other employees, and one of the masked men pointed at the night manager and said, "That's him."

The night manager was dragged into the restaurant office and told to open the safe. When he pretended that he couldn't, they whacked him on the head and threatened to shoot him. He instantly remembered how to open the safe and they left with $7,000.

Naturally, the police suspected that this was an inside job, since one of the robbers knew who the night manager was, where the safe was, and that it could be opened and would contain a considerable sum.

They began wondering: Could it have been someone like, say, Anthony, the ex-busboy? The problem was that because the men wore masks, there was no way to prove it had been Anthony, even if they could find him.

While they wondered what to do, they got lucky. A

tipster told them that the same guys who robbed the deli were going to knock off another Oak Park restaurant, Edwardo's.

So several Oak Park cops posed as customers and kitchen workers at Edwardo's and waited.

Sure enough, when the employee took out some garbage, there were the men in masks and surgical gloves. They barged in but were rudely surprised to find a bunch of cops there to greet them.

One of them bolted out the door and sprinted away. The cops chased him and they wrestled around a bit, and a gun went off.

"Oww," the masked man said, since the bullet had punctured his leg.

When they removed his mask, they found that their hunch had been right. It was Anthony, the ex-busboy.

The cops assumed that Anthony either took the busboy job in the first place just to case the restaurant or later decided that robbing the place paid better than filling water glasses.

In either case, he and his pals were charged with both robberies and are awaiting trial. Since they were caught on the spot it is assumed that even a Chicago judge will find them guilty of at least one of the robberies.

Anyway, that is what went through the mind of Mueller, the deli manager, when Anthony's unemployment comp papers came from the state.

And he said: "Hey, wait a minute. The reason he's unemployed is that he is a stick-up man."

So he called the state office and told them that he didn't think it was necessary to give money to someone who hits people on the head and points guns at them.

He was told that this did not disqualify Anthony from receiving jobless payments.

"They are eligible," a state employee said, "unless they are convicted of public aid fraud, not for just some crime. We don't deny someone just because they have a criminal record."

Mueller took the forms and dropped them in a can with half-eaten corned beef sandwiches.

When we mentioned this to a state welfare person, she said: "I don't understand why he wouldn't want to fill them out. We're just trying to verify information."

Incidentally, the reason Anthony is not in jail, and asking the state for walking-around money, is that he was able to post bond on the robbery charges. He plunked down $2,000 in cash.

No wonder the poor guy is broke.

A Tale of Two
Smut Merchants

August 1, 1984

In simpler times, there lived a neighborhood photographer near Armitage and Milwaukee on the Northwest Side.

He was self-employed, working weddings, anniversaries, graduations and other family events.

But he also padded his income with a line of goods he didn't advertise in the neighborhood paper. He sold nude photos, the kind that used to be called dirty pictures.

His model was usually his wife, an empty-faced woman who tended their second-floor flat and two small kids and did what her husband told her to do.

Other than having a big chest, there wasn't much to recommend her as a model, except that she was willing to take off her clothes and pose in embarrassingly revealing positions—usually with her tongue hanging out, which was supposed to lend an erotic effect.

The photographer would sell stacks of the wallet-size photos to guys he knew in factories and taverns, and they in turn would sell them to guys they knew. That's the way such things circulated in the days before porn stores and national smut magazines.

The people in the neighborhood didn't know about his dirty picture business because he went outside the neighborhood to sell them.

But then he made the mistake of asking a teenage girl from the next block if she would be interested in making some money as a model.

When he told her exactly what he had in mind, she told her mother. The mother told the father, who owned a corner tavern. And the father and his large son, carrying baseball bats, went to the photog's home and banged on the door.

Not being a dummy, he wouldn't open the door. So the father yelled that if he ever came near the girl again, they'd kill him. He added that one more mistake would get him dropped into a sewer.

A few weeks later, the local grammar school had its June graduation. The gym was filled with proud parents and grandparents and uncles and aunts.

The tavern keeper was there for the graduation of one of his other children.

During the ceremony, the tavern keeper glanced around and saw the photographer with a camera in his hand.

"What's that creep doing here?" he said.

It turned out that the creep was there as the official photographer of the graduation.

"He ain't taking my kid's picture," said the tavern keeper. And he got up and bashed the creep in the jaw.

"What are you doing?" the principal shrieked.

"He's a creep," the tavern keeper explained, knocking the photog to the floor.

"Stop," the principal cried.

"I'm almost done," he said, giving him a couple of kicks that sent him fleeing from the school.

The tavern keeper then explained to the other parents that he had driven a degenerate from their midst, so someone else was called to take the class picture.

And within two days, the photog had moved from the neighborhood and was never again seen.

I thought of that incident while watching Bob Guccione, owner of *Penthouse* magazine, being interviewed on a network news show about the controversial Miss America photos.

It occurred to me what remarkable changes have occurred in only a few decades.

That neighborhood pornographer was punched around and had to move away in disgrace.

In contrast, Guccione, a multimillionaire, wears gold chains, has corporate offices, travels the world in jets and is invited to the best parties in New York.

If the photog tried to explain why he did what he did, nobody would have cared. They would have just punched him some more.

But Guccione appears on network shows to speak with great seriousness about the journalistic necessity of publishing photos of two young women in lesbian poses in his magazine.

And there are people who take him seriously.

Actually, there's little difference between that neighborhood pornographer and Guccione, the magazine publisher, other than financial success.

The only significant difference is that the photog was born before his time.

Maybe. But I prefer to think that it was the tavern keeper, unfortunately, who was born before his time.

● 122

Some Numbers
Will Just Kill You

November 22, 1984

My sister sounded depressed. Earlier that day, she happened to drive past our mother's old house. "It's gone," she said. "It looks like it burned down."

That was no reason to feel bad, I told her. If anything the fire was a civic improvement.

The last time I was there, about two years ago, the house was still standing. But it had become an outpost for the Insane Idiots or some other such gang.

When I stopped my car and got out for a sentimental look, the various louts who were draped across the porch or hanging out the windows scattered like roaches. They apparently mistook me and a large friend for narcs.

I thought about the house and the neighborhood after listening to Mayor Harold Washington's number-jugglers try to justify cutting the size of the police department.

They say that in recent years, the city's population has been shrinking, while the police force has remained just as big as it used to be.

If you believe as they do—that in numbers there is truth and wisdom—it stands to reason that the police force should now get smaller.

But in the words of Inspector Wang, a fictional detective: "Only one thing wrong with your theory: It's stupid."

Consider the neighborhood I just mentioned, only a stone's throw from Humboldt Park. Or, as measured today, only a bomb's throw.

In all the years we lived there, I can remember only one street murder.

Oh, there was violence. Energetic tavern brawls.

123 ●

Post–softball game fights. Even neighborhood gang confrontations.

But nobody was killed. The worst damage was usually a split lip, a cracked tooth or a broken nose.

And we had our share of criminals. The neighborhood produced some of the city's leading career burglars and car thieves, although they usually went somewhere else to steal. Not out of community loyalty. There just weren't many diamond brooches to be found near California and North.

But in general, it was a safe neighborhood. Kids could wander around. Women could go to a store at night. A young guy and his girlfriend could take a stroll to the Crystal Theater on a warm summer evening. Teenagers could walk a few blocks over to the next neighborhood to get a hot dog from Nick the Greek's pushcart.

And on hot nights, something happened that now seems hard to believe: People slept in the park.

Nobody had air-conditioning. So hundreds of families would leave their sweltering flats, carrying blankets and pillows into the park, spread out on the grass and sleep until dawn.

Today, if you see somebody lying on the grass in Humboldt Park at 3 A.M., call the cops, the paramedics and the undertaker. He's surely got a blade in his ribs or a bullet in his bladder.

The whole area is now a war zone. The streets and alleys and parks and gangways and doorways belong to the Insane Idiots, the Deranged Disciples and the Latin Lunatics.

Nobody says "put up your dukes" anymore and settles for a bloody nose as the mark of victory. Step across the wrong street or give somebody the wrong salute and it's the fast draw and a bullet in the head.

On Friday or Saturday nights, the hospital emer-

124

gency rooms look like a scene out of "M*A*S*H." Except nobody is laughing.

When I was a kid, one cop could have taken care of the whole neighborhood. Now, one cop wouldn't be *safe* in the neighborhood.

It's not just Humboldt Park—it's big hunks of the entire city. Much of the South Side, the West Side, the long strip of meanness through the entire North Side.

Sure, the population has grown smaller. But it's also grown nastier. There are more guns in the hands of more crazies, young and old. The sociologists can try to explain why. What matters is that it has happened.

And if this city needs anything, it needs more, not fewer, cops on the street.

So pay no attention to the arguments of number-jugglers in City Hall. They can juggle all the numbers they want, but I'll give them a few numbers to remember:

He was 6′ 8″. Three gang punks stopped him on the street in broad daylight. One punk fired a .22. He lost ten liters of blood.

He was dead at seventeen.

I don't know how a smaller police force is going to get rid of those kinds of numbers.

Rude Awakening
for a Daydreamer

October 15, 1986

I suppose this story falls under the general category of: "In this town, it's every man, woman and child for themselves."

125 ●

It begins with Rose Ann Morales, thirty-one, a hair-stylist, waiting for the traffic light to change. She's listening to her car radio and daydreaming.

So she doesn't notice the young man step off the sidewalk and walk up to her car on the passenger side. Nor does she notice him take a gun from his jacket.

She sees him only when he uses the gun butt to smash her car window and reach in to snatch her purse from the car seat.

This is known as smash-and-grab, a form of theft common to some parts of the inner city.

And where Rose Ann was—in front of a public housing project—it's more common than kick the can.

Rose Ann screams. The young man strolls into a playlot, stops, turns and stands there looking at her.

Rose Ann looks around. It's broad daylight. Cars are moving along. A few people stand on the sidewalk waiting for a bus. Pedestrians walk by. It's a normal city scene.

Except a man with a gun has just smashed her car window, grabbed her purse and is coolly standing less than fifty feet away.

She rolls down her window and screams. "Help. That man just stole my purse."

A few people glance at her, but nobody responds.

She honks her horn and shouts some more.

A city garbage truck stops and the driver says: "What's wrong?"

"That man in the playlot, he just stole my purse."

"The one standing there?"

"Yes. He smashed my window with a gun."

"You say a gun?"

"Yes."

"I can't help you, lady. But I'll see if I can send back some cops."

And he drives on.

In the distance, Rose Ann sees the flashing light of an approaching police car. She thinks: It's coming to help me.

Rose Ann leans on her horn and waves her arm out the window. The policeman peers at her for a few moments. She blows the horn and waves again.

The policeman finally crosses the street to her car.

"That man just smashed my window and took my purse. He has a gun."

"Where?"

"That one, standing in the playlot."

The policeman looks just in time to see the thief disappear into the entrance of the towering project building.

"Can't do anything now," the policeman says.

"You can go catch him," says Rose Ann.

"No, once they get inside there, you can forget it. He could be anywhere in there."

"But he's got to either get on an elevator or go up the stairs. You can catch him."

She looks closer at the policeman. He's no kid and about fifty pounds overweight. She realizes that he's not about to hoof up stairs after a stolen purse.

A teenager walks up and asks what's going on.

"Do you live in there?" Rose Ann asks.

The teenager nods.

"A man stole my purse and went in there. If you can go in and find it, I'll give you a reward."

The teenager gives her a sly look. "If he stole your purse, where you gonna get the money?"

Rose Ann takes cash from the pocket of her slacks. "I never carry money in my purse. But there are personal things in it. I want them back."

Two other teenagers join them and the three discuss the possibility of finding the purse.

"Probably tossed it down the incinerator chute," one

of them says. "That's where they always throw them."

"Always?" Rose Ann asks.

"Yeah," one of the kids says. "They do that a lot."

"Get it back and I'll pay you."

"What's it worth to you?"

"I'll give you $20."

"Twenty each or just twenty?"

The cop says: "Look, kid, twenty bucks split three ways is more than any of you have got."

One of them says: "I could get real dirty messing around that trash."

But his friend says: "Yeah, but I can always wash up and I can use the money."

They go in the building. A few minutes later, they come out and say: "Lady, you're gonna have to tell us what your purse looks like. That thing's loaded with purses. We can't bring 'em all out."

"It's white and brown," she says.

They go back in. When they return, they hand her the purse and she gives them $20.

Her credit cards and checkbook are gone, but her personal papers are intact.

As he leaves, the policeman says: "You did the smart thing."

"What's that?" she asks.

"Not chasing him. He wanted you to chase him. A woman chased one of those guys into the building a few weeks ago. We brought her out on a stretcher."

Later, Rose Ann says: "You know, it was my own fault."

Why was it your fault?

"I shouldn't have been daydreaming."

The observation of a true city dweller. It makes me wonder if we shouldn't drop the old city's slogan—City in a Garden—and replace it with something more timely.

Something like: "Daydream at Your Own Risk."

Who Cares About
Rapists' Rights?

March 26, 1984

Since I'm of the opinion that rapists should be hanged—
and not necessarily by the neck—I can't generate a lot of
sympathy for the social conscience or ethnic awareness
of Aldo Mello and his irate friends.

Mr. Mello is one of the leaders of a Portuguese protest movement in New Bedford, Massachusetts. He and
others are trying to stir up compassion for the four barroom clods who recently were found guilty of raping a
woman on a pool table.

His effort appears to be showing results, judging from
the thousands of angry people who filled the streets for
a protest march. I don't think records on this sort of thing
are kept, but it appeared to be the biggest save-the-rapist
protest march in modern history.

Mr. Mello explained the logic of the protest by saying: "Our purpose is really to show the judge and the
country at large that we're together, that we oppose the
verdict, and we oppose the attack on our heritage."

That's not the dumbest thing I've ever heard, but it's
in the running.

The fact that Mr. Mello and his friends gathered in the
streets to show that they disagreed with the verdict doesn't
mean a thing. They weren't part of the jury that sat for
days and listened to every word of testimony and found
more than enough evidence to justify a guilty verdict.

The jury system is fallible. But it works a lot better
than getting secondhand information through TV, newspapers and radio talk shows, then stomping about the
streets and muttering about what an insult the verdict is
to one's ethnic pride.

And it's hard to see how jailing four men who appear to have received their sex education in a zoo is an insult to anybody's heritage. Is Mr. Mellow saying that it is part of the Portuguese heritage for groups of leering men to satisfy their romantic yearnings on a tavern pool table?

Nor is it clear how the guilty verdict can be interpreted as an attack on the heritage of the Portuguese, since the victim was Portuguese, the prosecutor was Portuguese and some of the jurors were Portuguese. If all those Portuguese are anti-Portuguese, then something even bigger than the rape trial is brewing in New Bedford. It could be a civil war.

Not too long ago, we passed through the era of modern protests. From the late 1950s through the early 1970s, just about anything worth protesting was protested.

There were marches for civil rights, students' rights, female rights, gay rights, the unborn's rights, Yugoslavian rights, Polish rights, Third World rights, children's rights, divorced men's rights, handicapped rights, Nazis' rights, leftist rights and rightist rights.

But this is the first protest march held on behalf of Portuguese rapists' rights. And it is the strangest display of ethnic pride that I've ever seen.

I grew up in a neighborhood that was mostly Polish, and—as in most ethnic neighborhoods of the time—there were suspicions of discrimination. I remember Slats Grobnik having grave doubts about the American Dream when he said:

"How come so many crooked politicians in the city are Irish? If we got a fair shake, I'm sure we could steal just as much as them."

But it never occurred to us to view the jailing of Polish-American criminals as an insult to the community. When the cops hauled some neighborhood thug off to the Wood Street station, most of us felt relieved that they got him before he got us.

Even the arrest of popular Polish criminals didn't bring about protest marches. Pops Panczko, for example.

Panczko, as some of you may remember, was for years Chicago's best-known thief. At least among those who did not hold elective office.

He was arrested thousands of times. It wasn't that he was incompetent. He was highly skilled. But he had that old-time work ethic, and he'd get up in the morning and go out and steal for ten or twelve hours, so the law of averages and the cops would occasionally catch up with him.

Sometimes he deserved being arrested, such as when some cop would come across Pops inside a fur store at 3 A.M. Sometimes he didn't, such as when a cop would come across Pops having coffee in an all-night restaurant and try to hit him up for a $50 unreturnable loan.

Most of the times he was arrested, he was found innocent, even though everybody—the cops, the judge and the jury—knew he did it. But it was hard to be mad at a guy who would testify with a straight face that he happened to be in a jewelry store at midnight because he had weak kidneys, the door was unlocked and he was just looking for the bathroom.

Eventually he was convicted and went to prison. But nobody marched in protest, even though Pops was a totally nonviolent criminal. Why, if Pops had ever encountered a lady on a pool table, he would have asked her to move so he could steal the pool balls.

So I think Mr. Mello and his friends in New Bedford should consider something else to protest. Complaining about cruelty to rapists isn't going to get them much support, outside of a few maximum security prisons.

Life Turns Mean
for Street People

November 26, 1984

It's always been common for some of those who have little money to try to pluck a little cash from those who happen to have some.

That's the motive behind most, although not all, routine street crime. Especially in the bigger cities.

Where you have a large poor population, it's inevitable that some young men will start eyeing the parts of town where the more affluent live or play and thinking about how pleasant it would be to have a small piece of all that disposable income.

The more bold or desperate do more than think. They drift over in the night and look for someone who appears to have a plump wallet, stick a gun to his nose or give his arm a few twists and maybe wind up with the price of a night on the town.

Those who have a less daring nature, but fast feet, might choose purse snatching over mugging. And the truly nonviolent thief will probably choose shoplifting as a career.

When Willie Sutton was asked why he robbed banks, he said, "Because that's where the money is." And the average mugger would probably give the same explanation for why he slams into a guy in a white shirt, a tie and shiny shoes.

It's a do-it-yourself redistribution of wealth. And most of the time there's nothing personal about it.

It happened in Dickens' London, old New York, Paris, Rome and every other city where the poor live near or among those who have money. It happens every day in Chicago and most other big cities.

But as we get more and more desperate poor, there's a greater gap between the haves and have-nots. And with TV advertising bombarding the have-nots with all the things they not only might have but—according to the advertising pitch—*should* have, the grabbers become nastier. They not only want what somebody else has, they get angry at him or her for having it. And that's when the gratuitous shooting, knifing or beating occurs.

And now we're seeing a new and weird twist to the struggle between the haves and have-nots. Like anything new and weird, it is happening in California.

In Santa Cruz, groups of well-off, middle-class young people have taken to attacking the less fortunate.

They call it "trollbusting." They even wear T-shirts showing some down-and-out person. Apparently the word *trollbusting* is some kind of play on the title of the movie *Ghostbusters.*

The targets of these youths are homeless street people—beggars, bag ladies, bag men, derelicts, the kind of people who are part of that growing population that lives in cardboard shelters, under bridges, in doorways or in a sanitation department salt box.

The existence of these people in their city offends the offspring of those who live in ranch homes.

So they've been threatening them, kicking them around and occasionally whacking them with baseball bats.

One young man, a twenty-year-old security guard, explained to a reporter why his friends are going in for bashing the poor and homeless.

"My friends resent the way the 'trolls' go begging around while they have to work and pay taxes. When you see people living off the money you work hard for, it makes you mad."

If that's the motive, it makes it about as senseless an act of cruelty as there can be. Most street people are among society's most independent members. They're getting little or nothing from the government, which is why they are living the way they do.

If these young goofs were sincere about defending their allegedly hard-earned money, they would be on the prowl for a four-star general or a defense contractor. Or one of the President's merry budgeteers.

A man who runs a free-lunch program for down-and-outers probably comes closer to a motive when he describes the poor-thumpers as "establishment middle-class kids who find it offensive that people don't conform to what they are. They want Santa Cruz to be some nice little rich town. This is something they get from their parents."

I'm not sure what's worse: somebody who is poor going out and robbing somebody who is well off, or somebody who is well off beating up somebody merely because he is poor.

But I do know what's safer. The Santa Cruz cops say they have not yet arrested anybody for assaulting street people.

Padded Cell 4

"Can't We Still Be Friends?"

If All's Fair in Love,
What About Later?

October 11, 1988

By writing this story, I am not condoning what Gerald did. His conduct was nasty, cruel and vindictive. But it was also funny, and with most of today's news being about the frantic babbling of politicians, anything with a chuckle is welcome.

Gerald lives in a suburb of St. Paul. He's divorced, and it is an understatement to say that he doesn't think much of his ex-wife.

That isn't uncommon, of course. Many divorced people loathe their former spouses. That's one of the reasons I almost never write about divorce disputes.

It's my experience that you ask a divorced person

137 ●

whose fault the breakup was, about 99 percent of the time the man will say "hers," and the woman will say "his." Depending on whom you talk to, in every shattered marriage there was one saint and one fiend.

Or, as an old divorce lawyer once told me: "They all lie. The secret of success is to get your client to tell better lies."

But to get back to Gerald and the nasty thing he did, as reported in the *St. Paul Dispatch*.

Gerald wasn't violent, as some ex-husbands are. There are countless cases of men beating up boyfriends of their ex-wives. And, although it is more rare, ex-wives have been known to pluck a few tufts of hair from an ex-husband's new flame.

There are tire slashings, obscene late-night phone calls and, occasionally, a guy will get sloshed and drive his car onto his old front porch.

Gerald, to his credit, showed a bit more wit and imagination.

After Gerald was divorced by Sharon, she packed up and moved to another state, while he remained at their old address.

One day a letter came for Sharon. The decent thing would have been for Gerald to send the letter on. But Gerald had bitterness in his heart, as many divorced people do.

So he opened and read the letter.

It turned out to be a questionnaire from someone in Sharon's old high school class of 1958.

This person was putting together a newsletter that was to be sent to the other members of the class, bringing them all up to date on what their old classmates were doing thirty years later.

Those readers with a malicious nature have already guessed what Gerald did.

Yes, Gerald filled in the answers to the questionnaire.

● 138

Then he signed Sharon's name and returned it to the person putting together the newsletter.

And a few months later, more than a hundred members of the class received the newsletter and read about each other. When they got to Sharon's responses, their jaws dropped.

There could be little doubt that Sharon sounded as if she had had the most interesting thirty years since graduation day.

In answer to "occupation," the answer was: "Retired on third husband's divorce settlement."

There was a question that asked: "Achievement most proud of":

The answer: "My three divorces and how each time I married into more money to the point where I am now living on the $400,000 settlement and interest from my third divorce."

Another question asked for an "outrageous, unusual or interesting experience."

The response: "Going out to Virginia . . . on my job and having an affair with two different guys while my third husband was back in Minnesota working two jobs."

But Gerald hadn't even hit his stride. For the question about hobbies, he wrote:

"Nightclubbing, partying and looking for new and wealthier husbands."

And for "Secret ambition or fantasy," he wrote:

"Seeing if I can't get married as many times as Liz Taylor and gain my riches through divorces, not work."

When Sharon finally saw the newsletter, she said "eek," or something to that effect. Then she called her lawyer.

And now Gerald has been slapped with a $50,000 lawsuit by Sharon. She says that's what it will cost to soothe her embarrassment and mental anguish.

I suppose that if there is a moral to this story, it is that it's a good idea to let sleeping ex-wives lie.

And Gerald had better hope that when this $50,000 case comes to court, he draws a judge who either has a wicked sense of humor or a nasty ex-wife.

Elevator Manners:
On Again, Off Again

April 6, 1988

The elevator door opened and the tiresome ritual began.

Those of the male persuasion stepped slightly to the side and just stood there.

Those of the female persuasion leaned tentatively forward until they were sure we weren't going to move.

Finally, one of them bolted into the elevator, followed by the others. We went next. But after all the hesitating, the door began to close and one of us had to bang it back open to get aboard.

The elevator went down, and at the first floor the door opened. The ritual was repeated. The males stood as if frozen until a female got off, followed by the others. Then the rest of us scrambled out before the door closed.

Why do men do it? Why do I do it? Why do we believe that we must let females get on and off elevators before we do?

It has been years since the historic first public bra burning. Since then, women have risen to high public office, become major corporate executives and work as equals in most professions and many trades.

True, many inequities remain. But even the most hard-nosed of feminists must concede that during the past two decades, great strides have been made. I know dozens of women who swear better than me.

Yet we persist in the elevator ritual, the opening-the-door-for-them ritual, the first-in-the-cab ritual, the stand-up-when-they-get-to-the-restaurant-table ritual, the help-them-on-with-their-coat ritual, the shake-hands-only-if-they-offer-to-first ritual and many others.

Why shouldn't I get on or off the elevator first if I'm closest to the door? It would be more orderly and result in less emotional stress brought on by those moments of indecision.

Even worse, on the few occasions that I've done it—bolting on or off the elevator with a devil-may-care attitude—why do I immediately feel guilty and embarrassed, fearing that the females behind me are thinking: What a boor.

Seeking answers to these questions, I asked a female executive why women expect to get on and off elevators first.

"We don't expect it," she snapped. "In fact, it infuriates me."

Then why do you do it?

"We don't do it. You do it. It's your fault. You stand there like a bunch of wimps. So if we don't break the logjam and get off first, we'll be riding the damn thing all day."

You mean you don't see this as being a courtesy required of men?

"Of course not. Who the hell cares who gets off the elevator first, unless it's on fire? And I don't need a man to open a door for me or help me on with my coat. I've been opening doors and putting on my own clothes as long as they have. And when they jump up at a restaurant table, one of them usually hits the table with his leg and slops water all over the place."

Then why do we do these things?

"How do I know? You're the ones who are doing it. We just wish you'd stop."

You won't think we're boors?

"Of course not. If anything, we'll respect you for treating us as equals and being enlightened."

I am always seeking enlightenment in this foggy world. But the question still remained: Why do we do it?

So I put that question to the eminent psychiatrist, Dr. I. M. Kookie.

"If I may summarize your question about elevators and doors and cars," he said, "what you seem to be asking me is, why do we continue to abide by the outmoded tradition of 'ladies first,' is that not correct?"

Yes. Is it because we are subconsciously patronizing them, treating them as weaker or lesser creatures?

"Possibly. But I believe that the primary psychological reason for our behavior is that by letting them go first, we get a real good look at their legs and their bottoms. I'm a leg and bottom guy, you know. And, boy oh boy, when you open a car door to let one of them out, you can sometimes get a glimpse of thigh."

That's why we do it, in order to gawk and leer?

"I don't know about you, but that's why I do it. I always help them on with their coats because it gives me a chance to get a sniff of their perfume. A real turn-on, I'll tell you."

Doctor, I am shocked and disgusted.

"You are? Then I'll tell you something. You ought to go see a psychiatrist."

Nonsensible Shoes
Women's Arch Foe

January 19, 1984

One thing this job has taught me is that no matter what I write, it's going to make somebody mad.

I'm sure that if a column consisted of nothing more than "Good morning, I hope you have a nice day," someone would respond:

"What do you mean, good morning? It was a *lousy* morning, you jerk." And somebody else would say: "I hate dopes like you who tell me to have a good day! I'll have any kind of day I want."

If I wrote nothing more than "God bless you," my phone would surely ring and somebody would shout: "I'm an atheist, so keep the blessings to yourself, chump!"

So I wasn't surprised when I received a letter from a lady named Diane, whose last name appears to be something like Bohenta, or Balenti. I can't be sure, because she was so angry that she scrawled it.

Diane had just finished reading my observations on Sunday's debate among the Democrats who are panting for the Oval Office.

In that column, I had written that the debate was the best I had ever seen because it didn't have the rigid, complicated rules imposed by the League of Women Voters, which usually runs major political debates. And the questioners weren't the usual collection of self-important Washington correspondents.

Now, even though I don't like the way it runs debates, I did say some nice things about the League of Women Voters. And I quote:

"This is a very fine organization, made up of upstanding ladies who wear sensible shoes and beige sweaters. It

143 ●

has high-minded goals and sincere public concerns."

I ask you: Is there anything in that paragraph that would cause you to froth at the lips and pound the table?

Of course not. But now comes Diane Whatsername, whose letter almost emits steam. She says:

"You have a hell of a lot of nerve and absolutely no room to make fun of the League of Women Voters—*or their shoes!*

"How dare you write about the kinds of shoes they wear? Did you watch yourself being interviewed last week on TV? Well, you certainly did not look the epitome of neatness.

"I don't like you a bit and will never read anything you write again.

"I am not a member of the League of Women Voters, but I think you owe them an apology—especially about their shoes!"

Absolutely not, Diane. Never. Not even if hell freezes over. I tell you now and I will tell you forever: I will never apologize to the League of Women Voters for saying that its members wear practical shoes.

What kind of wishy-washy character would I be if I took the forthright and bold position that they wear practical shoes, only to reverse myself a few days later and say they *don't* wear practical shoes?

Would you have me publicly snivel that I was mistaken—and that they wear overpriced spike heels, open toes and pointy toes, designed by some guy who looks like a gigolo?

No, I won't do it, and I'll give you another reason I won't: My comment on their shoes was meant to be complimentary.

I've always believed that the silliest thing most women do is wear shoes that crush their toes, twist their arches and make them walk like ducks.

● 144

Go in any restaurant at lunch and peek under the table and look at the feet of the women. (If a cop grabs you, tell him you're doing research.)

What will you see? You'll see women's shoes kicked off and the toes trying to wiggle away the pain.

But you won't see men doing it. That's because most men have the sense to buy shoes that don't make their toes hurt.

Walk down any downtown street and look at the women's feet. No matter how bitterly cold the weather is, you will see countless females wearing flimsy little shoes that require less leather than my billfold, their toes jutting into the slush.

But not once have I seen a man mincing through a snowbank with his toes sticking out of his shoes. Even an old bum has enough sense to stuff some paper in the holes.

Or listen to a group of women talk and eventually they will get around to their foot guys. They all have foot guys.

One will talk about how her foot guy is terrific at filing away calluses, and another will say that her foot guy is beyond compare at digging out corns and a third will say that her foot guy is unequaled at uncurling her toes.

Do you ever hear men talk about their foot guys? Of course not, because they don't put things on their feet that maim and maul them.

Stand outside the office of any foot guy and you'll seldom see a man. The sore-feet industry is supported almost entirely by women. Sometimes I wonder if the women's shoe designers aren't secretly in cahoots with the foot doctors.

It's strange that in an age when women are demanding equality, when they claim to be able to do almost anything a man can, when they say they are just as smart, practical and sensible as men, they routinely practice masochism on their own feet.

And I will never accept the argument that women are the equal of men until they liberate their toes.

Someday, a woman will run for president. Probably in my lifetime. When that happens, I'm going to go to her first press conference, but I'm not going to ask about economics, foreign relations or defense.

I'm going to ask the big question: "Do you intend to make your feet public?"

I hope Diane now realizes that there was no reason for her to get upset about that other column.

Or this one, either. I think.

It's Time That Men Started to Share

May 30, 1986

There can be no doubt that this country is facing a grave new domestic crisis. It's on the cover of *Newsweek* magazine, the front page of the *Wall Street Journal.* Even that most intellectual of publications, *People* magazine, has taken note.

I'm talking about the growing glut in America of unmarried women and the shortage of eligible men.

The crisis came to light when a scholarly study revealed that white, college-educated women who are still single at age thirty have only a 20 percent chance of getting hitched.

At thirty-five, only one out of twenty will ever marry. If they don't make it by forty, they can just about forget it.

How did this come about? Some say it's the fault of the modern yuppie female. They are too choosy.

As Pete Axthelm, the sportswriter, points out, you can look in the personals and never find an ad that sounds like this:

"Rich, witty and beautiful career woman—Craves balding, cigar-smoking sportswriter who enjoys hanging out until closing time in smoky saloons, picking up large dinner tabs and taking healthy and invigorating day trips to racetracks."

He may be right. I sometimes glance at the personals and they always say things like: "Single professional woman, 32, wants to meet single, professional man, 32 to 39½, tall, handsome, humorous, youthfully mature, energetic, sensitive, open, caring, who enjoys long walks on beaches, art, music, Woody Allen movies, cross-country skiing, scuba diving, tennis, gourmet dining, Sundays at the zoo, world travel, cats, foreign sports cars and restoring old mansions. No smokers, drinkers or bowlers need reply."

As Slats Grobnik put it: "If my old lady had been that fussy, she'd still be living with her ma and pa and working at the Jewel, instead of having the bliss of cooking my dinner and doing my laundry while I'm sitting here having this beer with you."

Those who blame the females for their own plight also say that yuppie materialism is at fault. The females, they say, were so busy with their careers and buying their own condos and Japanese cars that they didn't notice that the young men at the health club were being snatched off by those who were more alert.

But whatever the causes are, the studies have reportedly brought panic to millions of women. They are now said to be looking around for any eligible warm body.

At the same time, it has brought joy to yuppie men,

147

who now find themselves in even greater demand.

As one yuppie man told me: "This is terrific. I don't even have to pretend that I'm open and caring anymore."

Even nerds, wimps, fatties, baldies and geezers are being seen in a new light.

"I went in a singles bar the other day," a lifelong nerd related, "and an attractive yuppie female said to me: 'Do you like skiing in Aspen?' I said: 'No, I collect stamps.' She said: 'God, that's erotic.' "

But the experts say that even if the pool of previously unwanted males is tapped, the crisis will not be eased. There just aren't enough unmarried males, especially with so many men now holding hands.

So how is this nation to avoid a future filled with biddies who have only their cats for company?

The only sensible solution that I see is some form of polygamy.

I'm not saying that men should set up households with two, three or four wives, all living together. That's not practical. Too much squabbling over who uses the bathroom first. It might also prove physically exhausting for the man and cut into his golfing time.

But some form of time-sharing, as is done with vacation retreats, might work.

A man might be married to two women and spend alternate weeks with each of them. That's probably as much time as many men now spend with their wives, if you consider the demands of watching TV, having a drink after work and not talking after quarrels.

It would probably lead to more stable marriages and fewer divorces, because a couple would be ensured of regularly having a week apart to cool down from whatever they have been fighting about.

I mentioned my idea to a female, age thirty-two, professional, who likes long walks on the beach, skiing,

Woody Allen movies, world travel, Sundays at the zoo, etc., etc.

She said: "I think you are a jerk."

Huh! With that attitude, she'd better get used to her cats.

Now Admit It:
Men Hate Cats

February 20, 1984

An old friend invited me over to see his new condo and meet his new significant other, with whom he was trying to establish a new and lasting relationship.

After he opened my wine to let it breathe, he and I sat in the living room listening to his new Bang & Olufsen stereo ("state of the art in miniaturization," he said) while she went into the kitchen to prepare a new recipe for pasta primavera.

They had met, he said, on adjoining Nautilus machines. She was working on her thighs while he was trying to improve his pecs. One exercise led to another and there they were.

I was congratulating him on his good fortune when it walked slowly into the room. It arched its back and stared at me.

"You have a cat?" I said.

He nodded.

"But you have never been a cat person."

"Actually, it was hers. Now it is ours," he said.

"I thought you were allergic to cats."

"Yes, but I checked with an allergist. Turns out that

I'm allergic to long-hair cats. This is a short-hair, so it's okay."

"You never liked cats. You always told me you hated them."

"Shhh," he said, nodding toward the kitchen. "She might hear."

"Don't you think you should be honest about such things? You can't build a lasting relationship on deceit."

"I am honest. I like cats now. I really do. Look. We get along fine."

To prove his point, he scooped up the cat and rubbed it under the chin. It responded by digging its claws into his arm and biting his thumb.

"Feisty little thing," he said, dabbing the blood with a cocktail napkin.

Just then, she came in from the kitchen with yogurt and carrot sticks and said: "Oh, you've been playing with Yolanda."

He smiled and wiped away the rest of the blood.

"It attacked him," I said. "I think it was after an artery."

"Oh, it's just her way of playing."

"Really," I said. "Well, if that cat was as big as one of us, it would probably rip his throat out. And mine and probably yours. The only thing that prevents cats from killing us is that they're not big enough. But they'd love to."

She stared at me the way the cat had. She might have arched her back, too, but I couldn't tell because her jogging suit was loose.

"I gather you're not a cat person," she said.

"Of course I'm not. I am a man. Or a male person, as they now say."

"What has that to do with it?"

"Everything. Men don't like cats. Only women do. If you took an honest, scientific survey, you would find that

97.3 percent of all men dislike and distrust cats. Probably more, but you know how some people lie to pollsters."

"I don't believe that," she said. "I've known lots of men who like cats. Most of them do."

"No. What you have known are men who lie about their feelings toward cats."

"Why would they lie?"

"To please women. They know that you like cats, so they pretend to like them, too. It is all part of the wimping of America."

"The what?"

"The conversion of normal males into wimps. This cat thing is just another facet of it. Movies like *Tootsie*. Guys like Alda. And the proliferation of cats as America's most popular pets. Take my friend here."

"Leave me out of this," he said.

"No. We must be open and honest. Now, would you have had this new and hopefully lasting relationship if he had said: 'You have a cat? Hey, I hate cats. If that sneaky thing comes near me, I'll toss it out the window'?"

"Of course not," she said. "But he would never have said anything like that because he likes cats. You do, don't you?"

"Yes, yes, I love them," he said, patting the cat's head and yanking his hand away before it could shred his fingers.

"No," I said, "he likes dogs. Most men like dogs. It's an instinct going back beyond the dawn of history, when man lived in caves and his first four-legged friend, besides his significant other, was his dog. It was a faithful dog who helped him catch game and who guarded the entrance of the cave and drove away the fearful beasties that lurked out there in the darkness—including big man-eating cats. Throughout history, men have had their dogs. You never read stories about cats rescuing lost people or driving off bandits or wolves. And in the movies, the only men who

151 ●

like cats are the villains. Would movies lie?"

She looked at my friend and said menacingly: "Be honest, because our relationship depends on it. Do you really prefer dogs?"

"Of course not," he yelped. "I hate dogs. Big, smelly things. Barking all the time. Ruining the rugs. Cats, I love cats."

I decided to skip the pasta and let myself out. The last thing I saw was my friend trying to tickle the cat behind the ears.

And it was trying to pluck out his eye.

Modern Romance in for a Hairy Time

March 18, 1987

Sometime this year, thousands of men will begin rubbing a chemical into their scalps twice a day at an annual cost of about $600 each. They'll do this in the hope that they can avoid becoming bald.

And a certain number of them will grow hair. Tests have shown that the amazing new product can indeed cause hair to sprout.

Not for everybody. The chemical seems to be most effective for men who are younger, in their twenties and thirties. But the main thing is that it works, and this is the first time anything has been found that grows hair.

So that means that in the future, we will have fewer bald men in this country.

The question is, so what?

Will they be happier? Will their lives be richer and

152

fuller? Will they achieve otherwise unattainable goals?

The answer is probably no.

If men were honest, they would admit that it is their hope that the presence of hair on their heads will lead to their ultimate goal: making out with female persons.

Despite what anyone might say, that is the single greatest motive for a young man's dread of a receding hairline or the appearance of a thin spot on top of his noggin.

Thinning hair or a bald spot doesn't prevent anyone from being a great surgeon, a rich pork-bellies trader, a hitter of home runs, a Nobel Prize–winning mathematician, a world-renowned orchestra conductor, a rock star, an airline pilot, an Oscar-winning movie actor or a competent tuck pointer.

Hair is really irrelevant. The fact is, we don't need it. It's something nature provided countless centuries ago to keep us warm when we came out of the cave. But as man and his environment have evolved, it's become merely decorative. And in many ways, we're better off without it.

At a club where I go to get a little exercise, I sometimes watch those with great wads of hair go through their postshower ritual. I know one young guy who spends at least fifteen minutes using a blower and brush to dry and shape his locks. I'm sure there are hundreds of thousands of men who do the same thing.

He works out at least three times a week. That means that he spends forty-five minutes a week doing his hair—and that's only in the club locker room. I assume he does the same at home the other four days. That's another sixty minutes. Or a total of 105 minutes a week.

A little simple arithmetic shows that he could spend ninety-one hours a year just doing his hair. That's assuming he does it only once a day. That comes to almost four full days a year.

So let us also assume that he retains enough hair and vanity to continue this practice for another twenty years, until he is in his mid-forties.

That means he will devote the equivalent of eighty days of his life just blowing hot hair at his hair and primping it with a comb or brush. Almost three months.

And if you break it down into eight-hour work days, it becomes an even more awesome number. It is the same as 240 days on the job—forty-eight work weeks. Almost a year, minus vacations and holidays.

All that, just in the hope that some female creature will admire his blow-dried tresses and say: "Your place or mine?"

But what if she says "Beat it, creep"? A whole year of his life will have been wasted.

And that's quite possible, because his potential success is based almost entirely on the availability of female creatures who happen to be dimwitted enough to have their hearts go aflutter over a man's cranial hair.

But what if he should have the misfortune to run into nothing but modern, enlightened women—those brainy females who judge a man by his wit, his knowledge, his willingness to share, his decency, compassion, understanding, accomplishments and net worth?

Then the poor hairy booby has blown a year tending his noggin and is out of luck.

Despite this, I don't want to discourage anyone from doing anything they think will improve their romantic life. If you believe it is worth the effort to rub that stuff in your scalp, do it.

And maybe in a year or two, you'll have as thick and luxuriant a growth as some primate in the zoo.

But you couldn't have picked a worse time to take advantage of this scientific breakthrough.

There you'll be—with your blow-dried, razor cut,

chemically induced curls hanging over your ears and collar.

And what will she probably say?

"Uh, you don't happen to have the results of your latest medical test handy, do you?"

Padded Cell 5

"Can't We Play for Fun?"

Brits' Scorn
for McEnroe a Riot

May 31, 1985

In the past, many Americans have felt embarrassed by the rude behavior of John McEnroe when he has played tennis at Wimbledon in England.

He has used foul language, abused the officials, made obscene gestures at the fans, kicked the grass, pouted and shouted. Once he even swatted a ball at a line judge, hitting the bloke's bald spot.

Although he's done the same things in this country, it seemed much worse in England. That's because the English have an image of being so, well, so civilized, so sensitive to unsportsmanlike behavior.

And they have reacted with dyspeptic indignation.

The English press has described McEnroe as nothing less than a thug, a barbarian and—even worse—as a cheeky sort of fellow. English government officials harrumphed that he not be permitted to play at the hallowed Wimbledon tournament.

Their tennis officials have fined him thousands of dollars. They even went so far as to deny him membership in the All England Lawn Tennis Club, the first singles champion in 104 years to be snubbed.

In this country, many Americans shook their heads and felt sheepish. That's because many of us feel inferior to the English—at least in the social graces.

They have this precise yet languid way of speaking. They never seem to lose their poise. Even if you're a head taller, they manage to look down their thin, patrician noses at you. And they *do* take high tea.

Well, I say to hell with them and their haughty airs. And I hope that the next time John McEnroe plays at Wimbledon, he demands an apology for the past criticism.

If he doesn't get it, he should go to center court, drop his whites and moon the entire stadium.

Where, I ask, do the English get off berating a kid from New York for a few cuss words, an extended middle finger and bit of spouting and pouting?

As a rude lad, he's just a piker, a twit, a mere nuisance.

For world-class unsportsmanlike behavior, I offer you the murderous British soccer fans.

When they get upset, nobody tallies up the swear words. Instead, there's a body count. And at last count in Belgium, the number of dead—trampled when the Brit fans attacked the Italian fans—was thirty-eight.

And the amazing thing is that there's no reason to be surprised. Horrified and disgusted, sure. But surprised?

Not at all. On a less grand scale, this has become standard conduct for English soccer fans.

Whenever there is a big match in England—or an English team plays on the continent—it is usually preceded by a full-blown riot in the streets.

Then, during the actual game, there is maiming and mauling in the stands.

And, after the game, win or lose, there is another full-blown riot in the streets.

Now, I'm not talking about the kind of rowdiness that occurs in this country after a World Series. In comparison, we are mere pussycats.

An English judge recently sent twenty-five fans to prison for showing their displeasure with another fan's loyalties. They slashed his throat with a broken bottle and then mauled a cop who tried to interfere.

At another match, the fans bashed each other about the streets. Before the festivities ended, eighty were hurt. Almost a hundred cops were hurt. And the fans managed to knock down a brick wall that fell on a fifteen-year-old bystander and crushed his brain beyond repair.

In this country, fans entering a stadium might be asked to show the contents of a bag to make sure they aren't bringing in their own booze. But in England, they frisk them for knives, razor blades, railroad spikes, lead pipes, brass knuckles, whips and chains. I guess waving a team banner is too tame for them.

And these are the same people who sneer at John McEnroe for conking a line judge with a rubber ball.

Next time, John, spit in his eye. The one without the monocle.

Spring Training
Hits a New High

March 7, 1986

When the month of March rolls around, I sometimes wonder whatever happened to the phenom.

You remember the phenom, don't you? Or maybe you're too young.

The phenom was a creature that existed in the daily news dispatches that were filed from Arizona, Florida, California and other sunny places where baseball players went to soak the off-season booze and fat from their bodies and prepare for another season.

And in almost every spring training camp, there was at least one young player, up from the minors, who qualified as a genuine phenom.

He, the young phenom, was what made March and spring training a special time of year for those of us who were filled with hope—or gullibility—about the coming season.

We would sit in the cold Northern cities and read daily reports about the phenom. How he was hammering balls awesome distances over the fences, over the palm trees, over the trailer courts and into some distant drainage ditch.

"The kid hit one today that had to be 550 feet, and it went right through the wall of a warehouse," said Manager Lunk Hedd. "He's got muscles in his ears."

"The kid made a throw from deepest center field that didn't rise more than eight feet off the ground and it hit the catcher right in the mitt and knocked him all the way to the backstop. The kid has an arm like a bazooka," said Coach Biggie Gutt, "only it bends."

"When he runs, he reminds me of a gazelle," said scout Ben Zadrine. "He even nibbles leaves from bushes."

"All the tools . . . he can't miss . . . the greatest prospect since . . . and he writes home to his mudder every day."

It was the phenom who helped make the month of March less the tail end of winter and more the beginning of spring. When the phenom started hitting the blue darts or whipping blinding fastballs past helpless hitters, we knew that summer was on its way.

Of course, we seldom ever saw the phenom in the flesh. Sometime near the end of spring training, somebody would be unkind enough to whip a curveball over the outside corner at the knees, causing the phenom to spin like a top. After that, it was just a matter of packing his bag and heading for another season in Chattanooga.

But that was okay. While the phenom lasted, he was fun to read about. And every so often, one would actually make it to Opening Day.

Now, though, what invigorating news do we have from spring training? Name me even one phenom who can hit balls into the distant cactus plants.

No, what we get now are stories that concern the burning issue of whether baseball players should agree to urinate regularly into little bottles.

Or whether some players should surrender portions of their paychecks as punishment for having once sniffed white powder that made them say "Oh, wow."

Where once we read about a phenom racing to deepest center field, leaping ten feet into the air and catching the ball between his thumb and forefinger, we get debates on whether grown men should be required to make wee-wee into a bottle once a week, once a month or between times at bat.

163 ●

We read about agents decrying violations of their clients' constitutional right to the privacy of their urine content.

It used to be that a sportswriter need only to know how to mark a scorecard to cover spring training. Now he needs a degree in constitutional law and maybe one in pharmacology.

So the days of blissful reading about spring training are gone. No more phenoms to capture our imagination and give us the joy of even a false hope.

But who knows? Maybe we will eventually get a new kind of spring training phenom.

"This kid has got it all," says manager Lou Bodomy. "His nasal membranes are intact. Not one needle mark on his arms or legs.

"And he's got the most terrific urine we've seen in twenty years."

Why America Was Left Out in the Cold

February 17, 1988

Many Americans are disappointed and depressed by our poor showing in the Winter Olympics. As a patriotic friend told me: "It seems like everybody who wins a medal has a name that sounds like a brand of vodka."

But if you think about it, there's no reason to feel that way. There are two valid reasons why we're losing, and we don't have to apologize for either.

First, the most obvious, our best athletes aren't involved in these games. They're not dummies. Why waste time learning to steer a sled with their feet while lying on their backs when they can make millions of dollars hitting a baseball, dunking a basketball or catching a football?

Beyond that, though, is the fact that the Winter Olympics are rigged against the United States. And I don't just mean the figure-skating judges, some of whom are kinkier than any Chicago judge.

It's the sports themselves. These are not the winter pastimes in which Americans participate on a regular basis. Who do you know that rides a luge or a bobsled or jumps 300 feet on a pair of wooden slats?

True, many Americans go to ski resorts, but most of their time is spent in the lodge bar looking for someone with whom to have safe sex.

Some of us ice skate, but we're not obsessed with it the way the various scandihoovians are. If Hans Brinker had been an American youth in need of transportation, he wouldn't have been puffing around on a pair of skates. He'd have gone out and stolen a car.

If the Olympics were fair, they'd include our cold-weather pastimes, and we would walk away with a sack of medals.

For example, there should be a snowblower event, or several of them. The short competition would be for sidewalks. The longer, more grueling event would be sidewalks, driveways, alleys and side entrances.

The scores would be based not only on speed but on displaying proper form, which would include how much of your snow you flung onto your neighbor's property.

Another event would be snowmobiling. Once again, there would be two categories—straight-line snowmobiling and northern Wisconsin snowmobiling.

The second part of this event—the northern Wisconsin slalom—would be the most challenging because it would require that the snowmobile drivers consume a pint and a half of Monarch Brandy and six beer chasers before racing in the dark of night over hill and dale, between utility poles and trees, in and out of ditches, through patios and backyards and under wire fences before reaching the finish line with their heads still attached to their shoulders and being able to walk unaided from their machine without falling down or throwing up.

Another exciting event would be battery-cable jumping, which is tremendously popular in northern inner-city neighborhoods. We could send a crack team made up entirely of men who are somebody's brother-in-law. I don't know why, but throughout the history of battery-jumping, the top cable jumpers have always been somebody's brother-in-law. You never hear somebody say: "My battery is dead. I'll call my cousin (or uncle or father or neighbor), because he's got cables." It's always "I'll call my brother-in-law." Sociologists should study this.

And there could be an event called Marathon Sub-zero Bus Stop Waiting, which could be dominated by Chicagoans. The contestants would be judged on how long they can wait without freezing to death, as well as on their form. The form points would be given for style shown when stepping off the curb and peering hopelessly into the distance, and for obscene muttering.

Another event—which would draw contestants from neighborhoods in such icy cities as Milwaukee, Chicago, Detroit and Buffalo—could be called Staggering Home. Instead of a starting gun, the race would begin with someone with an apron shouting "Closing time, last call," and the contestants would stagger out into the cold and make their way over a slalom course consisting of ice patches, snowbanks, slush puddles and abandoned cars, all the while being pelted with sleet, hail and blinding snow while searching their pockets to see whether they can find their house keys so as not to awaken the little lady. Style points would be awarded for how well they negotiate the front steps on all fours.

The best part of my Olympic proposals is that reporters would not only be able to cover the competition, many of us could also take part. And win.

Addressing Soccer Question Head-On

June 30, 1986

A former resident of a Latin American country called and asked me why most people in the United States are so indifferent to the world's biggest sports event, the World Cup of Soccer.

"I have been in this country for one year, and I am amazed that the people here don't know anything about this game. It is the most popular game everywhere else in the world. But here, it is nothing.

"I don't understand this because you are such sports fans. In the place where I work, I hear people talk about sports more than anything else. Everywhere I go, I hear people talk about sports.

"But it is always baseball or football or basketball, never soccer. When I mention soccer to them, they don't even know how it is played. I have told some of them it is the most popular game in the world, and they don't even believe me. They think the Super Bowl is important. They don't know that most of the world doesn't know what a 'Refrigerator' Perry is.

"How did this country—how can I say it—lose touch with the rest of the world?"

He's right, of course. Most of us don't care about soccer. And I'm not sure I care why we don't care. What we need is less sports hysteria, not more.

But he does raise an interesting question that's been

answered many times by sports experts, psychologists and bartenders.

Most of them agree that we don't care about soccer because it's not something we played when we were kids. So, when we grow up and become soft and fat and our livers expand, we want to watch games from our youth, so we can identify with the players and fantasize that we're out there on the field.

The exception is horse racing, of course. Nobody identifies with a horse, unless they, too, have crude toilet habits.

The reason we didn't play soccer as kids, the experts say, is that when this country was young and developing, it rejected much of what was left behind in the Old World and developed its own popular games—baseball, basketball and football.

And guns. The pioneers needed guns to shoot animals, Indians and each other. So today, we follow part of that tradition and still keep guns to shoot animals and each other. Mostly each other.

True, soccer is being played more in many schools, especially as many parents wise up about football and the prospect of having a household filled with gimp-kneed sons. And there's professional soccer, although most of the fans talk like the wild and crazy Bulgarian brothers from the old *Saturday Night Live* shows.

But soccer is still a minor sport. And my friend Slats Grobnik has his own theory on why it will always be so.

As Slats puts it: "It's a question of dignity."

In what way?

"You look at our big sports and what the heroic moments are. In baseball, it's when a slugger swings and there's a loud crack of the bat and the ball goes sailing way over the fence. Or when the pitcher rears back and whips the ball past the hitter for a strikeout.

"In football, it's when a wide receiver goes running

down the field and the quarterback heaves a long bomb and the guy grabs it in stride and races into the end zone.

"And in basketball, it's when some guy flies into the air, spins around twice, switches the ball from one hand to another and slams it into the hoop.

"But in soccer, the big moment is when some guy with stumpy legs bounces the ball off his head into the goal.

"Now, think about that: using your head to hit a ball. That's not heroic. It's undignified.

"In our popular sports, what do we do if a ball bounces off somebody's head—an outfielder or a pass receiver or a point guard? We laugh at them because it looks goofy. Except in bowling, where we'd have to bury him.

"And I'm glad we don't play soccer, because I don't think it's good for your health."

But it is great exercise.

"Maybe. But have you ever noticed how most guys from Latin America are a lot shorter than us?"

What has soccer got to do with it?

"All that hitting the ball with their heads. It compresses their spines."

New York Golf Offers Slice of Real Life

July 12, 1985

As an occasional golfer, it's always seemed to me that the designs of most golf courses in this country are all wrong.

Unlike the ancient golf courses in Scotland, where golf was born, ours are not natural. That's especially true

169 ●

of the hazards, which make a golf course challenging.

In Scotland, the hazards are natural. The sea, the dunes, the roll of the land, the thick weeds are all part of the original terrain.

In other words, a Scottish golf course looks like Scotland.

But can that be said about our courses? Are sand bunkers natural to Chicago? Or big and little ponds and winding streams? Rolling hills?

Of course not. They're man-made, artificial.

So I was pleased to discover that in at least one part of this country, there are golf courses with hazards that truly reflect the natural environment.

These are the thirteen municipal golf courses of New York City.

If you read the *New York Times,* you might have come across a recent report on the unusual hazards of that city's courses. For those who didn't, I'll summarize it.

After hitting a tee shot, a New Yorker might walk down the fairway and exclaim, "Drat, I'm in a hazard!"

A bunker? Not especially. It could be the trunk of an abandoned stolen car. They're dumped on the courses all the time.

Later in the round, he might say: "I think I have an unplayable lie. Do I get a free lift from there?"

A cart path? No. It could be that the ball had landed on or near a sleeping wino, many of whom snooze about the fairway and rough.

Or in the tent of one of the many vagrants who call the course home.

Or it might have even come to rest on a corpse. Those who have an urgent need to dispose of corpses frequently choose the golf courses for this purpose.

(The article didn't say what the rule is for a ball on or near a wino. Do you drop it two club lengths away? Or two bottle lengths? In the case of the corpse, do you move the ball or move the body? Is a casual corpse considered the same as casual water?)

But those are just examples of the stationary hazards. The movable hazards are what give the courses their true character.

For example, you get out of your golf cart and walk to the green to putt.

After putting, you look up and see your cart, with bag and clubs, fading into the distance, being driven toward the streets of Queens by some enterprising urchin.

Or you might be walking along a fairway and see somebody emerge from a bush.

When confronting a stranger, golfers, a friendly lot, will usually say, "Hello," or "Nice day," or "How you hitting them?" or something of the sort.

But it's possible that he'd put his hand in his pocket and say: "Your money, sucker. And the watch. And the ring. And the ball, if it ain't cut."

New York golfers have returned home after a Sunday round and said: "Honey, you should have seen it. I really had it going until the sixteenth hole. I was a cinch to break ninety. Then it all came apart."

"You sliced one?"

"No. This guy said he'd slice *me.*"

That's why some New York golfers carry more than an extra wedge or a seven-wood in their bags. Some carry cans of Mace or pistols. A few bring companions to stroll along with them—such as mean dogs.

Unusual questions of etiquette have arisen on New York courses.

When delayed by a slow group ahead, it's acceptable to ask politely if you can play through.

But is there a tactful way to ask to play through a couple of rival gangs having a brawl in your fairway? (I suppose you could use flattery and say: "My, you have a fine, smooth stroke, young man. Excellent follow-through. Tell me, what is the swing-weight of that piece of chain?")

Lately, the hazards have been somewhat reduced by new management of the courses.

But they still retain much of their natural appeal. And the odds for a hole-in-one are much greater than for a hole in the head.

President's Case
of Locker Jaw

October 29, 1985

I'm not sure which President of the United States began the practice of phoning locker rooms after games to congratulate victorious athletes.

It definitely wasn't Calvin Coolidge or Herbert Hoover. For some reason I think it might have been Richard Nixon. Or maybe Nixon was the first to call a locker room to try to fix a game.

But whoever started the tradition, this past World Series has made it clear that the time has come to stop.

For one thing, the novelty value is gone. In the beginning, a President phoning a locker room and his conversation being broadcast to the world was something that caused people sitting in front of their TV sets to say "Oh, my goodness, Nora, isn't that something? The President is actually talking to Left McSpeed. Say, I wonder if they had an office pool in the White House."

Now it has become just another part of the postgame ritual, as predictable as the champagne being poured on heads and some ego-tripping franchise owner saying what a happy family he has created.

And with more and more sports on TV, Presidents have taken to calling more and more locker rooms. It's now expected after the World Series, the Super Bowl, the basketball championship and assorted college bowl games. What's next? Soccer? Bowling?

Worst of all, though, the players and managers no longer seem to be aware that they're talking to the President of the United States, the leader of the free world, the most powerful man on Earth, the top banana, the big enchilada.

In the early days of the White House-to-locker room hook-ups, the players and managers gave the appearance of appreciating the solemnity of the moment.

They would look properly respectful as they listened, phone to ear, while the President said something like:

"Lefty, this is the President speaking."

"Yes, Mr. President."

"I want to congratulate you on a great victory over a worthy opponent. You are a credit to the game, an example to the nation, and a blah, blah, blah for all the blah, blah, blah."

"Thank you, Mr. President. We're mighty proud."

"And the nation is proud of you and your team, Lefty."

"And we're proud of the nation, Mr. President."

"And I'm proud of you and the nation, Lefty."

"And I'm proud that you and the nation are proud of us, Mr. President."

"Thank you, Lefty."

"Thank you, Mr. President."

But now, as the conversation Sunday night demonstrated, the President barely squeezes in a word.

There he was in the White House, drowsily waiting

173 ●

around in his pajamas for the game to finally end so he could get some sleep.

His writers had prepared his congratulatory message, as well as some observations on the game to give the impression that he had actually watched it. And a few small jokes to show that he can be one of the boys, ha-ha. And when the phone call went through and the network was hooked up, he was ready to do his thing.

Instead, the manager interrupted to babble about what a fine bunch of dedicated guys he had on the team— as if for $1 million a year to play bat and ball they should be anything but dedicated. And the star pitcher interrupted what appeared to be the beginning of a witty presidential remark to giddily yammer at length about his wife giving birth.

They said the same things to the President that they would have said to any yahoo with a microphone in his hand.

As a result, Reagan sounded befuddled and never got to finish his remarks.

And when the President's call ended, I almost expected to hear the players say "Hey, who was that— Howard Cosell?"

That's no way to treat a President, even a President who sounded half asleep.

So in the future, I hope he and his successors will stop calling locker rooms, or at least pass along the chore to an assistant. And the message should be kept short and simple. Something like:

"This is the head of the federal Drug Enforcement Office calling on behalf of the President. He says congratulations. And I say don't pour anything in your nose."

Double Standard
Puts Odd Man Out

January 25, 1988

I once spent an evening playing poker with Jimmy "the Greek" Snyder. He lost and I won, so I can't help being a little fond of him.

One of the things I remember about that card game was that he seldom stopped talking. He didn't always make sense, but his ramblings were almost nonstop. Anecdotes about athletes and other gamblers, minilectures on how poker should be played and frequent grabs for the phone to place bets with his bookie.

For a while I thought it was a ploy to distract the rest of us. But as his stack of chips shrunk, I realized he was simply a compulsive talker. And being something of a celebrity, he felt obliged to dazzle us with what he thought was wit and worldliness, even when we yawned.

When the game ended and we split up, one of the other players expressed surprise that a professional gambler could lose to the likes of me.

I told him it proved one thing: Although it appears to be a simple game, poker requires some thought. And it was clear that Jimmy couldn't think and talk at the same time.

And this lack of brain-mouth coordination finally did him in. Somebody shoved a microphone in his face and he talked but didn't think.

By now, just about everybody knows what he said: that blacks are superior athletes because of selective breeding by slave owners and that if blacks become coaches, whites won't have any jobs in pro football.

Historians promptly said his breeding theory was nonsense, blacks said his coaching statement was racist

175 ●

and CBS said he didn't work there any more.

And this provided most of the nation's commentators, editorialists, cartoonists and some politicians with the opportunity to express shock, horror and disapproval at what they saw as evidence that ignorance and racism exist even in such lofty citadels of intellectualism as the football broadcast booth.

In other words, everybody had a great time. As they should. It was a wonderful farce.

Consider some of the comic elements:

Not knowing what hit him, Jimmy the Greek made a public apology, and to dramatize the depths of his remorse, he rushed to Jesse Jackson to seek forgiveness.

Naturally, Jackson was gracious and compassionate, which was to be expected of a presidential candidate grabbing some free network TV time.

So there we saw the humbled and grateful Jimmy being granted limited forgiveness by a statesmanlike Jesse Jackson.

This, of course, was the same Jackson who once referred to New York, which has a sizable Jewish population, as Hymietown.

And if that's not farce, I wasted many a Saturday afternoon watching the *Three Stooges.*

I'm not defending Jimmy the Greek. I'm sure he'll survive, if he stays out of poker games.

But in his own bumbling way, Jimmy the Greek had been trying to be complimentary to black athletes by talking about their athletic skills and how hard they work to excel.

That he was wrong in his explanation, even though he thought he was right, shouldn't be a surprise. He's a professional gambler and babbler, not a historian, anthropologist, sociologist or geneticist. And people in those rackets aren't sure why Walter Payton was so good, either.

● 176

In contrast, there wasn't anything remotely complimentary about Jackson's Hymietown remark. It wasn't as if he goofily mused: "I wonder why Albert Einstein and those other Jewish scientists got so smart. Do you think they eat lots of brain food like fish?"

What Snyder said about blacks was dumb. What Jackson said about Jews was nasty. To even come close to matching Jackson, Snyder would have had to have referred to Detroit or Oakland as Coontown.

Yet Snyder, who is nothing but an overblown bookie, has been kicked around by the same pro-Jackson commentators who had no problem explaining that Jackson's Hymietown remark was the result of an unfortunate cultural experience and social deprivation. Do they think that Jimmy the Greek went to Amherst?

I'm not sure what any of this means except that we apparently hold Greek bookies and black presidential candidates to different intellectual standards. We expect more of the bookie.

Ridiculous?
You Look Mahvelous

September 3, 1985

As the Labor Day weekend was beginning, I ran into Slats Grobnik on the street. He was on his way to engage in some end-of-summer recreational activities. And he was quite a sight.

"Well, how do I look?" he asked, turning around to show off his softball uniform.

Across the blazing orange shirt that covered his stooped back and scrawny chest was the name "Eddie and Theresa's Tavern" in bright blue lettering. Under that was the joint's address, business hours, phone number and the words: "Homemade chili, sandwiches, fair prices, no credit or checks."

His paunch sagged over the top of the orange softball pants, which tapered to his knees, revealing his storklike legs.

Dingy gray athletic socks sagged around his bony ankles. And his little toe protruded from a hole in his softball shoe.

"I cut a hole in it," he said, pointing at the shoe, "because I got a corn. That's why I always slide head first. I don't have corns on my ears."

Atop his head was an old fedora with the front brim turned up.

What's wrong with your fingers?

He held up his hands. On the left, his forefinger was taped to his middle finger. On the right hand, his ring finger was taped to his little finger.

"They're kind of messed up from getting hit with balls. They don't work too good separated, but they're okay this way."

"So," he repeated, "how do I look?"

I had to be honest, so I told him he looked ridiculous.

"Wha?" he said.

Look at yourself. Your hair, what little remains, is gray. You have dark bags under your eyes, your face is a mass of wrinkles, your body looks like something from a distant planet and you run like a duck.

"Well, you don't look like that Sylvester Salami yourself," he said.

True, but I'm not there running around a dusty softball field, pretending I'm still young. Slats, when will you accept that you are no longer a kid? Give it up. Act your age.

"Pete Rose is no kid and he ain't giving it up."

Pete is a professional athlete and makes a million dollars a year.

"Yeah, well, I made more than $118 this season in side bets, and we still got the playoffs left. Besides, if I don't play softball, what will I do all summer?"

Do something that is more in keeping with your advancing years. What about golf?

"I tried it once. First time up, I hit a ball that would have been a perfect double over the first baseman's head. It hit the pro shop window, and some guy in pink polyester shirt and pants comes out and yells at me, so I quit right there."

Well, there ought to be something you can do.

"Like what? You want to go out and play kick the can for a while?"

Nobody plays kick the can.

"That's right. So you want to go climb the back of a billboard, all the way to the top, and sit up there and spit and get people on the sidewalk mad?"

Don't be ridiculous. We'd break our necks.

"Awright, then how about we get some guys together, steal a little lumber, some nails and put up a clubhouse in an empty lot? Then we can dig a hole, make a fire, wrap up some potatoes in tin foil, cover it up and let them cook."

Yes, that was always fun, but I think we're past the age of building clubhouses.

"Sure. So what about going junking in the alleys? Remember when we found that broken radio? And the broken record player? And the broken sewing machine? We didn't have to do any Christmas shopping that year. If we find something good, we could take it over to Stanley's Junk Shop and get the price of a chocolate malt at Mr. Novak's Drug Store."

Stanley's shop is a condo building. Mr. Novak's store is a gas station. Besides, we'd look like suspicious characters, junking in alleys.

"And we can't go collecting bottles for the two-cent deposit at the grocery store."

No. It's all disposable cans or plastic now.

"So, the summer's almost over. And we haven't done much, have we? We haven't had much fun."

He picked up his scarred old softball bat, his six-pack of beer and said: "I got to go. Game's gonna start."

Then he looked at my button-down shirt, striped tie, single-breasted suit, shiny black shoes and said:

"You know something—*you* look kind of ridiculous."

Drug Trial's
Got Nothing on Ball

September 11, 1985

"Next witness."

"What is your name?"

"Lefty McSpeed."

"Mr. McSpeed, what is your occupation?"

"I am a major-league baseball player."

"And have you ever used cocaine?"

"Have you?"

"Please answer the question."

"I'll answer yours if you'll answer mine. C'mon, have *you* ever used it? Or smoked grass?"

"That is not relevant."

"Sure it is. Admit it—a lot more lawyers than professional ballplayers snort coke and smoke grass. That's because there are tens of thousands of you, but only a few hundred of us. The law of averages, right? So what's the big deal if I snorted a couple of years ago?"

"Ah, so you do admit to having used cocaine?"

"Sure. Hey, have you ever thought about looking into drug use by doctors? Holy smoke, I saw a TV documentary once that really popped my eyes. There are doctors who are half zapped most of the time. Wow, can you imagine having some guy who's all strung out checking out your prostate?"

"We are not here to discuss the medical profession."

"Well, you ought to be. If I get high, so what? Worst that can happen is a ball lands on my head. But you wouldn't get the kind of headlines from a doctor that you get from me, right? I mean, I hit .298 and had twenty-five home runs last season, and you just don't find doctors or lawyers with those kinds of stats."

"That has nothing to do with it. Now, did you ever observe any of your fellow ballplayers using cocaine?"

"Sure. And have you ever observed any of your fellow lawyers doing it? You ever go to a party and get offered a snort? Or a hit off a joint?"

"I told you, that is not relevant."

"It ought to be. I mean, there are tons of that stuff coming into this country every year, and if ballplayers are the only ones sniffing it, we'd have to have noses like elephants."

"I ask you to give us the names of the ballplayers you saw using it."

"Sure. And how about if you give me the names of some of your friends? What about your broker? I hear that some of those guys, especially the commodities guys who hit the big bucks, do more sniffing and snorting than a hound dog."

"That profession isn't on trial."

"Of course it isn't. Nobody's profession is on trial except mine. What about the guys who drive those big

181 ●

trucks on the interstates? I hear some of them use all kinds of goofiness pills to keep themselves going. If I get a little scrambled, maybe I throw to the wrong base. If one of them gets unhinged, he'll flatten three cars before he even gets his foot on the brake. So why aren't you talking to them? Afraid of the Teamsters?"

"If you keep this up, Lefty, you could be held in contempt."

"Well, I'll be honest: I do feel a certain contempt. This country has been openly doing drugs for the last twenty years, and this is the first time one occupation has been singled out. I think maybe somebody is getting high on headlines."

"Your Honor, will you order the witness to answer my questions?"

"Oh, boy, now I'm getting it from a judge. Not one ballplayer has been accused of fixing a game since 1919, but I'm always reading about judges fixing cases. So how come I'm sitting down here and you're sitting up there? All I did was put a little powder in my nose—I didn't put a bag of money under my robes."

"Lefty, are you ashamed of what you did? Do you regret your adventures with an illegal substance? Do you publicly renounce your evil ways?"

"If it makes you happy, sure, I'll go along with that. But do you regret the malice that is in your heart? The hunger for headlines, the envy of my salary, the desire to humiliate me and others in order to further your public career?"

"I caution you—"

"And what about that fellow sitting there taking notes—the well-known writer who has been heaping contempt on us in his articles? Does he regret the three times he got nailed for drunken driving and called his pal, the police chief, to get him off the hook? Or when he hired a

●   182

crooked alderman to be his lawyer? Hah! Get him up on the witness stand and grill him about hypocrisy."

"Lefty, you are a disgrace to a great American game."

"How can you say that? I thought that what we're doing here was playing a great American game."

Baseball Justice
Just a Swing Away

August 5, 1987

While I was watching a baseball game, an incident occurred that made me question why this sport, above all others, is considered the great American pastime.

In this particular game, the pitcher was obviously agitated because things hadn't been going too well. It was his own fault, of course, since he was an incompetent.

So he reared back, let fly and the ball sped toward the batter's head.

The batter sprawled in the dirt, and the ball missed conking him by only a matter of inches.

When he got up, he shouted a few obscenities at the pitcher. Then he took one step forward, as if thinking about getting out to the mound and wrestling a bit.

The umpire stepped forward, waggled a finger at the batter and warned him not to do any such thing. And the game resumed.

It was an example of pure injustice.

Here you had a batter, doing what the rules and his paycheck require him to do: trying to hit a ball thrown by the pitcher.

The pitcher's job is to try to make the batter swing

183 ●

and miss the ball or hit it to one of the fielders.

Instead, the pitcher threw the ball in the general direction of the batter's brain.

Now, the rules don't say the pitcher should throw the ball at the batter's brain. That's not how you get the batter out. That's how you kill someone. Even worse, if struck in the head, the batter could be permanently impaired and become a sports broadcaster.

But who had a finger of authority waggled at him? Who was warned by the enforcer of the rules to restrain himself and be nonviolent?

Not the pitcher, who was the assailant in this incident, but the batter, who was the intended victim.

What kind of system of justice is that?

In no other sport does such unfairness exist. In football or boxing or hockey, if somebody tries to knock you down, you or your teammates are allowed to knock them down. In most sports, if somebody does something sneaky and unsportsmanlike, the offender is punished—not the victim.

But in baseball, it's just the opposite. Recently, a cowardly cur from the San Diego Padres threw a ball that hit Andre Dawson of the Cubs in the face.

For several long moments, the spectators weren't sure if Dawson was alive or dead. When he finally regained consciousness, his reaction was perfectly normal and justified. He got up and went looking for the guy who had bloodied his face.

Naturally, the lotus-eater ran away and hid in the locker room.

And when order was restored, who was punished? The person who had flung a deadly missile at someone else's head?

Not at all. It was announced that the sneak had left the playing field by his own choice or that of his manager.

But for the crime of trying to retaliate in a manly

184

way, Dawson was officially ejected from the game by the umpire.

Some of the philosophers who broadcast baseball games try to justify this inequity by saying that the "brushback pitch" is part of baseball. That is what they call a ball thrown ninety miles an hour in the general direction of someone's nose—a "brushback pitch."

But I've looked through the rules of baseball. There is nothing that says it is the pitcher's right or duty to use a ball as a deadly weapon.

I also asked a prosecutor how the law would react if someone was walking down the street and someone else threw a hard object that hit him in the face and spilled his blood.

He said: "We'd go after him for assault, a felony, which can carry with it a prison sentence."

I also asked what the law would say if the victim, dripping blood, pummeled his assailant.

"He would be perfectly justified," the prosecutor said.

So it's clear that the rules of baseball should be changed to conform with those of an occasionally civilized society.

I suggest something I call the Cavarretta Response.

Some of you may recall Phil Cavarretta, a native Chicagoan who was once a Cub star.

One day, I was at a game when a pitcher threw the ball at Cavarretta's head. He ducked and survived.

But on the next pitch, he swung. The bat somehow slipped from his hands and whirled right at the pitcher's head. The pitcher dived to the ground, narrowly avoiding decapitation. The pitcher didn't throw at anybody's head again that day.

This response should be made part of baseball's official rules: "If a pitcher throws a ball that forces a batter to fall down to avoid being struck in the head, the batter may, during the course of the game, fling his bat at the pitcher's head."

It would not only be fair, but it would make the sport more entertaining.

But as it stands now, there might be something in what the Russians say about their having invented the game.

Big Bucks Sink Joys
of Fishing

September 28, 1984

The first time I saw one of them, I was sitting in a small tin boat, anchored in a quiet cove on a sprawling lake in Arkansas.

A friend and I were fishing. That means we were half asleep in the shade of a tree, with a couple of lines dangling worms in the water. Every so often, one of us would snap open a can of beer, study the puffy clouds drifting across the blue sky, check the worm's health, then doze off again.

Suddenly, we heard the terrible howl of a big piston engine. And into our quiet cove roared a low, sleek boat doing about sixty miles an hour. It bounced across the water, did a sharp turn and the motor went silent.

It was unlike any fishing boat I had ever seen. It seemed to be covered with sparkledust and was equipped with all sorts of electronic equipment. It had the names of fishing-equipment makers written all over the side.

In it were two men wearing jumpsuits and long-billed caps. No sooner had the engine been turned off than they began whipping casts near the shoreline. They would cast and furiously crank the reel. Over and over, they cast and cranked.

After a few minutes, they started the engine and went roaring away. But a little later, we heard a distant sound that became louder and louder, and another boat barreled into our cove. Once again, the two occupants flailed the water with dozens of rapid-fire casts before speeding away.

"What the heck is going on?" I asked my fishing partner.

"I don't know," he said, "but they must be nuts. That's no way to fish. They don't even have time for a can of beer."

Later, we discovered that what we were seeing was a professional bass fishing tournament. All over the lake that day were high-powered bass boats, equipped with everything from depth sounders to cigarette lighters.

Dozens of good old boys named Billy Bob and Willie Joe were trying to catch enough bass to grab a hunk of the $50,000 prize money.

And they were fishing in a way I had never seen anybody fish. Instead of doing the sensible thing, which is to anchor in a restful spot, toss a worm or minnow over the side, sip a can of beer, admire the sky, observe a circling hawk and catch a few winks, they were rushing about in a frenzy.

They'd stay in a spot for only a few minutes, hammering the shoreline with casts. Then they'd speed away to another spot.

At the end of the day, they'd roar into the marina and turn in their fish, which would be weighed. And the guy with the heaviest catch would be the winner.

That was about fifteen years ago. Since then, professional bass fishing has become a big-time sport. Tournaments are held all over the South and Southwest. Professional bass fishermen trailer their boats from one lake to another. And all over the country, ordinary fishermen emulate them by buying powerful boats, with swivel chairs, electronic equipment and sophisticated rods and reels.

But I still think my friend was right when he said that was no way to fish. Certain pastimes lend themselves to professional competition. Fishing isn't one of them. If there is any sport that is meant to be done slowly and relaxed, it is fishing. Huck Finn and Tom Sawyer knew how to fish. Feet up, eyes closed. Lazy. No competition.

And no greed.

I mention greed because it turns out that the world of professional bass fishing now has a big scandal. Some of the fishermen worked out a scheme to give them the edge in catching the fattest bass.

They would go to Florida, where the biggest bass are found, catch some, keep them alive in fish tanks and take them to the Louisiana or Texas lake where the next tournament was to be held. Then they would sneak the fish into the water of some cove or inlet and return to that spot when the tournament was being held. The fish, being dumb creatures of habit, would still be hanging around. And, being dumb, they would let themselves be caught again.

Various federal agencies are investigating. One former champion apparently killed himself after he was called to testify before a grand jury. There are reports of death threats against witnesses. And now, nobody knows which fish to trust.

It's hard to believe that an act as simple as catching a fish could wind up being the object of a grand jury investigation.

I'll stay with the old cane pole. And pass the beer cooler, please.

● 188

Modern Men Can't Deal with Poker

December 12, 1986

The poker sharks of Las Vegas are scratching their heads over a stunning development in their series of world championship tournaments.

One of the big-money tournaments has been won by a woman. And in another, a woman finished in fourth place.

Because poker, at least at the shark level, always has been a male-dominated game, the professionals are asking why women are suddenly becoming a force.

I think I know the answer. In fact, I saw the change coming years ago, and the success of women in this tournament just proves that I was right.

Having played poker most of my life, I've noticed that fewer and fewer men under the age of forty know the game. And those who do play are easy marks.

There are two reasons for this.

First, this country ended the military draft. Young men were no longer forced to serve two years in the Army. Or to rush off and join the Navy or Air Force to avoid sleeping in a foxhole.

The barracks used to be where a young man learned to play poker. The instructors were usually Southern-born career noncoms who were patient, understanding and willing to pluck a young recruit of everything but his teeth.

And when the game ended, they'd count their winnings and kindly offer to loan their penniless victims enough to buy smokes and beer until the next pay call. At 10 percent interest.

Unless he was completely stupid, a young man eventually learned not to draw to inside straights, not to let his Adam's apple jiggle when he was concealing a full house and to politely decline free snorts from a tequila bottle passed around by somebody named Tex.

Beginning with World War II, through Korea, during the peacetime draft of the 1950s and early '60s, and into the Vietnam years, the military produced several generations of poker players. They ranged from the competent to the expert, from those comfortable in a kitchen nickel-dime game to those who could hold their own at pot limit in a tavern basement.

Then the draft was ended. And millions of young men no longer spent those formidable years sitting around a footlocker, wondering whether Sarge really had that fifth spade in his down cards.

Instead, they stayed home and ingested strange herbs and spices and turned their energies to revolution—mainly, the sexual revolution.

Then came another social development that discouraged the playing of poker. The modern American male fell madly in love with his own body.

It began with jogging. Then came such games as racquetball. And this led to fascination with Nautilus and other muscle-building devices.

There were even young men who joined aerobic dance classes, the dears.

Those who panted, grunted and sweated justified their labors by saying things like: "My body is a temple; I must not desecrate it."

But what they really had in mind was: "Hi, my name's Brad. Do you come here often? Really? My place or yours?"

A physical fitness obsession is in total conflict with the playing of poker. To play poker, you must be willing to sit in one place for hour after hour, until the Saturday dawn creeps through the window. You must be willing to sit in a smoke-filled room and eat midnight meals of salami and Swiss, pickles and beer. That's not the ideal training routine for building more attractive pecs and lats.

Then there are the video games and the home computer. These are what many young men, who in another age would have been learning poker, now play. A pity. Some of the gifted hackers who use their computers to break into banks, swindle credit card companies or change the grades of an entire graduating class would have been talented players of Texas hold 'em.

So the recent success of women in professional poker doesn't mean that women are becoming better players. There always have been some skilled female players. But they're being noticed now because there are fewer and fewer good male players.

It's all because the draft ended. And as time passes, poker will be a game played only by a few old coots in small-town American Legion halls.

The rest of the country will be sitting in front of the TV set or jiggling a video game.

It's a depressing thought. So if you want to see poker remain as part of our culture—the game of the Old West, the Army barracks and the tavern basement—then join me in trying to save it.

Write to your congressman and tell him to change the law so your kid will be drafted when he's eighteen.

Really, it will help make him a well-rounded person.

Play the Ponies, Pay the Piper

July 26, 1985

A few sportsmen were idling at the end of the bar and excitedly talking about the two guys who had just won almost a million and a half in the Super Bet at a local racetrack.

This led to recollections of their own triumphs, when one of them hit big on a daily double, another collected on a 40-to-1 shot and another won enough in one day for a luxury vacation in the Wisconsin Dells.

I listened quietly until one of them asked, "What's the most you ever won on a horse?"

I mumbled something into my beer.

"I didn't hear you," he said.

In almost a whisper, I repeated what I had mumbled.

They stared at me for a while, then one of them said, "You have never bet on a horse?"

Never.

"Not in your whole life?"

"What do you do when you go to the track? Just watch?"

It was a difficult thing to admit, but I've never been inside a racetrack.

One of them shook his head and said, "I never knew you were the kind of stiff who's against gambling."

Against gambling? I was taught poker at age twelve by an aunt who was a professional dealer, and I once played Texas hold 'em with Amarillo Slim and five-card draw with Jimmy the Greek. I've played pinochle with old-time Chicago firemen, craps with swarthy fellows in a Cicero basement, roulette at Monte Carlo and baccarat at the great casino of Baden-Baden, West Germany.

I've bet on myself in bowling, softball, fishing, golf, penny pitching and beer drinking and have squandered my children's inheritance on the Cubs.

However, I recouped most of my losses because I once knew a wealthy but hopelessly insane Republican who regularly bet me that his candidate would beat Richard J. Daley.

My motto has always been: "I'll bet any man from

any land any amount he can count in any game he can name." (I learned that from my grandmother, a bingo sharpie.)

"But why won't you bet on a horse?" one of the idlers said.

It goes back to my childhood. My father owned a neighborhood tavern and, as was the custom of the time, also took bets on horses.

"He was a bookie?"

In a very small way. My father couldn't afford to cover any big losses, so most of the bets were laid off with Nick, a big Mafia bookie. As a lad, it was my job to carry the bets in a brown paper bag to the cocktail lounge run as a front by Nick.

"Ah, so you were morally offended by the Mafia connection."

Not at all. In fact, I liked Nick. He would always tip me four bits and tell me not to spend it all in one place.

"Then what was it?"

I noticed that Nick the bookie wore silk shirts, a genuine Panama hat and a big pinky ring, had a season box at Cubs park and drove a long, black Packard. But the guys who placed the bets in my old man's tavern wore frayed work pants and painter's caps, had ring around the collar, rode the streetcar and sat in the bleachers, and their wives came around the bar on Fridays and screamed at them for blowing the paycheck.

"Ah, so you decided at an early age that horse players were suckers."

Something like that.

"Then you should have been a bookie."

I paused a moment, then said, "For one brief, shining moment, I was a bookie."

And it's true. It was a Saturday in May 1980, and a friend and I were in a big bar and restaurant in my neighborhood.

It was Derby Day, so everybody in the bar was talking about the approaching race. One of the many waitresses said, "Gee, I wish I could bet on it."

Remembering Nick, and feeling sly, I said: "I'll take your bet. I'll take anybody's action."

So, using the odds published in the newspaper, I began booking bets, even though I didn't have the slightest idea which horse was which.

And the bets rolled in. Especially from the waitresses, the female bartender, the female cashier and a couple of female customers.

I noticed a strange pattern. They were all betting on the same horse.

Everybody watched on TV as the horses sprang from the gate. And when it ended, the waitresses and other females screamed with joy and rushed over to collect.

"That was the year . . ." one of the idlers began.

Yes, that was the year a horse named Genuine Risk became the first filly since 1915 to win the Derby. And all those idiotic females, who knew nothing about racing, made sisterhood bets on her.

"You must have lost a tidy sum. She paid about $25 to win."

No, she paid $28.60 to win. The following Monday, I had to rush to the bank and tap one of my children's college funds just to cover the checks.

"Well," one of the idlers said, "that explains why you aren't a horse player."

Yes, and also why I became a male chauvinist pig.

Padded Cell 6

"My Fellow Americans, I Give You . . ."

Gary Hart Is Still
the Odd Man Out

July 20, 1988

ATLANTA—Even from behind, the tall figure was easy to recognize. Shoulders scrunched up, thick graying hair neatly blow-dried, suit elegantly cut.

Gary Hart was walking alone through a hotel corridor toward a bar and restaurant.

There was nothing remarkable about his being there. Except the fact that at that very moment, only a few blocks away, the Democratic convention was beginning.

Most of the big Democrats were in the convention hall. But Gary Hart was walking into the almost-deserted barroom and joining a few acquaintances in a booth.

Politics is a nutty business. Little more than a year

ago, he was the biggest Democrat of them all. Going toward the primaries, his lead in all the polls was enormous and growing. He was far better known than the other hopefuls, his campaign organization was enthusiastic and running smoothly, and he seemed a cinch to wind up with the nomination.

All he had to do was avoid screwing up.

As we all know, he didn't. The *Miami Herald* got a sleazy tip, followed it up with a sloppy stakeout and came up with evidence that wouldn't hold up in any divorce court in the land. And almost overnight, Hart went from being a potential president to the butt of David Letterman's gags.

Now the Democrats are anointing Michael Dukakis, whom almost nobody outside of his home state had heard of a year ago, while Hart sits in a hotel bar and glances at a TV set. Yet Dukakis, even though he is from Boston and tries hard, can't do nearly as effective an imitation of Jack Kennedy as Hart does.

In a way, it doesn't seem fair. Is what Hart did so terrible? Not really. Kennedy was using bimbos even while in the White House. His press pals knew but didn't tattle. The rumors about Jesse Jackson have been going around for years, but nobody stakes out his bedroom. So why did Hart get the shaft?

It was just the luck of the draw. If an editor at the Miami paper says "Hey, we're not Peeping Toms," it's Hart being followed this week by the army of camera-toters. He's up there, being hailed as the second coming of Roosevelt, Truman, Kennedy, blah, blah, blah.

Instead, as the hailing began, he was sitting in a hotel bar, watching the hoopla on the tube.

Not only is politics a nutty business, but many of the people who make it their trade are a bit strange. Hart among them.

You would think that after what Hart has been

through, he wouldn't come within a thousand miles of Atlanta this week. Would you? Would any normal person? Would you want gawkers pointing at you and saying: "Look, the best-known philanderer in American history."

Of course not. You'd be home, front door locked, watching your own TV. You might have to endure your wife's cold stares, but that beats being gawked at.

Yet he's here. And it isn't because he has to be here. He's not a delegate. He has no official role in this convention. If anything, most Democrats wish he would go away. He's an embarrassment to them. Many cringe at the mention of his name.

He could be back home in Colorado, humming about a Rocky Mountain high and enjoying the cool air. Instead, he's in one of the hottest, muggiest cities in America, with people pointing at him and saying: "Boy, that Donna really looked great in tight jeans. I wonder what . . ."

But he's here because he actually wants to be here. To provide himself with an excuse, he has hired on as a columnist for a chain of newspapers.

How's that for sick irony? It was a newspaper that destroyed his very genuine chance to become President of the United States. Those were columnists and other opinion-spouters who put him on trial and found him guilty.

And now, in order to wander the fringes of this political ritual, he's become one of those who did him in.

It reminds me of a scene in the Steve Martin comedy *The Jerk*.

Martin, the jerk, is talking to a potential girlfriend. The conversation goes something like this:

"When you and your boyfriend make love, could you think of me?"

"Maybe."

"Or if you and me make love, you could think of him."

"Maybe. Or you and him could make love, and you could think of me."

The jerk nods and says: "I just want to be in there somewhere."

That's Hart. He just wants to be in here, somewhere. If not as the candidate to be the forty-first President of this country, then with a notebook in his pocket and a press pass dangling from his neck.

As I left the hotel bar to go to the convention hall, Hart and his friends got up from their booth. But instead of going to the hall, they went to a table to have dinner.

Okay, I'll satisfy your curiosity. No, there wasn't a real looker in the bunch.

GOP Tries to Keep
Old Liberal in Closet

October 28, 1988

Slats Grobnik looked puzzled as he asked: "What ever happened to Abe Lincoln?"

Lincoln? He's still on Mount Rushmore. Why do you ask?

"Well, has he kind of fallen into disgrace or something? You know, like in Russia, where they kick old leaders out of the history books and take down their statues."

Of course not. Honest Abe is revered, one of the two or three greatest Presidents in our history.

"That's what I always thought. But something funny is going on."

Such as?

"Like this news story I just read where President

Reagan makes a speech about what a great guy Harry Truman was."

I read that.

"And isn't he always talking about what a great guy Franklin Roosevelt was?"

Oh, he's very fond of FDR.

"And I read where Danny Quayle said something good about Truman. And so did Bush. And I think Bush said something nice about FDR, too."

Yes, they've spoken highly of them.

"Well, maybe I missed something, but I thought Truman and Roosevelt were Democrats."

Of course they were.

"Then how come all these Republicans keep dropping their names? Why don't they talk about Republican Presidents?"

Now that you mention it, that is curious.

"I mean, I can see why they don't want to talk about Nixon, because he got kicked out of office. Or about Hoover, because he started the Great Depression. Or Coolidge, because most people don't know who the heck he was. But wasn't Abe Lincoln the father of their party?"

That he was.

"Then why don't they ever mention him?"

It's probably just an oversight.

"I don't think so. Nowadays, with all those sharpies who run campaigns, there's a reason for everything. And there's gotta be a reason why Honest Abe is getting the silent treatment."

I can't think of any.

"Come on, let's figure it out. Like Sherlock Holmes and Watson. Let's look for clues."

All right, what are the clues?

"Well, what was Lincoln most famous for?"

He preserved the Union by winning the Civil War.

"Hah! Now we're getting somewhere."

I don't understand.

"It's elementary, my stupid Watson. The Republicans want to win the South, don't they?"

Of course. It's essential to their battle plan.

"So what happens if Bush or Reagan or Quayle go down to Georgia to make a speech and they say: 'Remember, my fellow Americans, we are the Party of Lincoln?' "

There might be a certain coolness.

"A coolness? Hey, the audience is going to jump up and yell: 'You damn Yankee carpetbagger, don't you know that Lincoln sent General Sherman through here and burned up my great-grandpa's house in Atlanta?' "

That's quite possible.

"You bet it is. You go down South and start talking about Lincoln and guys named Bubba are gonna grab their shotguns and set their hounds on you. You ever notice who they name streets and highways after down there?"

Who?

"Not Lincoln or President Grant, I'll tell you that. Everywhere you go, it's Jefferson Davis Boulevard, Jefferson Davis Highway. He's still their guy."

You may have something.

"Okay, what else is Lincoln famous for?"

Everybody knows that. He freed the slaves.

"Right. So you think Reagan and Bush and Quayle want to remind white voters about that?"

But it was one of Lincoln's noblest achievements.

"Sure, but it's not something they want to mention in a 1988 campaign. If Bush gets up and says: 'My friends, we are the Party of Lincoln, the great man who freed the slaves,' you know what some white Southerner is gonna say, or some white guy in a bungalow in Chicago or Cleveland?"

What?

"They're gonna say: 'Oh, yeah? Then Lincoln's worse than Dukakis. Dukakis only let that Willie Horton out on furlough. Lincoln turned the whole mess of them loose and now they're moving into my neighborhood.' "

I suppose it's possible that some might react that way.

"Possible? Lemme tell ya, if the Republicans went around saying: 'Fellow Americans, vote for us because we are the Party of Lincoln, the man who won the Civil War and freed the slaves,' you know what would happen? Dukakis would get 70 percent of the vote. Even Lincoln's first name would hurt them."

His first name?

"Yeah, Abe. Some people would think he was Jewish, and they'd lose the anti-Semite vote."

An interesting analysis. I wonder what Lincoln would say if he came back to life today?

"I don't know what Lincoln would say, but I know what Reagan and Bush and Quayle would say."

What?

"They'd say: 'Look, another liberal.' "

Today Khadafy,
Next Month . . .

March 26, 1986

The great heavyweight fighter Joe Louis once embarked on what was called his "Bum of the Month" tour.

This meant that once a month, or more often, Louis would slap around an unknown pug who wasn't really tough enough or skilled enough to be in the ring with him.

He did it because there were so very few fighters really worthy of fighting Louis.

So to make money in those pre-TV days, stay in shape and remind the sporting world that he was the best, Louis took on whoever was available.

He fought more than a hundred such fights, in places like Topeka, Kansas; Waycross, Georgia; Odessa, Texas; and Moline, Illinois.

Because his opponents were such second-raters—who ever heard of Sugar Lip Anderson?—the fights weren't even official title bouts. They were labeled exhibitions.

But the crowd had a good time. And the local fighter would be able to brag that he once had the honor of being knocked senseless by Joe Louis.

It seems to me that this country has found itself in a position similar to that of Joe Louis.

Just as Louis had the physical ability to demolish anyone who challenged him, we have the military power to do the same.

We could, if we wished, blow up the entire world and everybody on it, including ourselves. Or we could single out one small part of the world and just erase it.

Who is as strong? The Soviet Union, maybe. But it's not convenient for either of us to settle the question. At least not at the moment.

As strong as we are, though, there seems to be a need in many of us to remind others of our strength. And to remind ourselves.

That's why there was such heartfelt pride and jubilation when we roared into Grenada and defeated a swarm of Cuban construction workers.

And it's the reason there's almost unanimous support in Congress, and probably among the American people, for the way we've been zapping those Libyan patrol boats this week.

●   204

The appealing thing about both adventures is that they aren't full-scale wars, which we don't want to get involved in right now.

We're calling the Libyan action a "confrontation." I don't recall what we named the Grenada invasion.

In that way, they're similar to Joe Louis' Bum of the Month fights, which were pushover exhibitions. The patrol boats from Libya are pushovers, as were the construction workers on Grenada. There is no risk of our losing, and they serve as military exhibitions.

When you think about it, we said we sent our planes over the Gulf of Sidra as part of a military exercise. What better exercise could there be than sinking a few patrol boats and bombing a couple of radar sites?

So what I'm suggesting is that President Reagan give some thought to adopting the old Joe Louis' Bum of the Month tour as part of our national policy.

Moammar Khadafy surely isn't the only national leader who has been making a pest of himself. And Libya isn't the only relatively small country that has been unfriendly to us.

Look at a map of the world. They're all over the place. You can't even pronounce many of their names, the foreigners.

I'm not saying that we should just go in and start shooting missiles at them for no reason. Nor should we do anything to provoke them into attacking us. As Larry Speakes, the White House spokesman, says: That's not why we went into the Gulf of Sidra. We just needed the exercise. And in this fitness-conscious age, who would deny us our exercise?

But I'm sure there are a lot of little countries that, if we gave them an opportunity, would be willing to do something to provoke us. That's all those pugs were doing when they climbed in the ring with Joe Louis—taking advantage of a rare opportunity to go up against the best.

What did it cost them, really? A few cuts and bruises, and maybe a broken nose, all for a lifetime of memories.

And what's it costing Khadafy? A few small boats. A few missiles. A few dozen of his citizens. All for the acclaim of his Arab friends and the world's many crazies.

So I think President Reagan, whether he knows it or not, is on to something that could become quite popular: his version of the old Bum of the Month tour.

The crowds will love it. But I'm sure, as a natural-born crowd pleaser, he already knows that.

A Bilgeful
from the White House

November 26, 1986

While expressing dismay with the most recent Iran arms disclosures, Senator Robert Byrd made a startling accusation.

Byrd said, "The President does not know what is going on in the basement of the White House."

I found that hard to believe, so I phoned a White House spokesman and asked if it could be true.

"Absolutely," said the spokesman.

Do you mean to say the President didn't know what Admiral John Poindexter and Lieutenant Colonel Oliver North were doing in the White House basement?

"Correct."

That's shocking.

"Not at all," the spokesman said. "Let me ask you this: Do you know what's going on in your own basement at this very moment?"

Well, no, I guess I don't.

"There could be hordes of ants running around your basement floor, and you wouldn't know it, right?"

I suppose so.

"You could have a pesky leak in the laundry room faucet and you wouldn't know it, right?"

That's possible.

"See? The fact is, most people don't always know what's going on in their basements. Especially in a big house like this one. Have you seen the size of this basement? You could get lost down there and never find your old tennis racket or golf clubs."

But what did the President think Poindexter and North were doing in the White House basement?

"I believe the President thought Poindexter was working on the sump pump."

The sump pump?

"Yes. Haven't you ever had any problems with your sump pump?"

From time to time.

"Of course you have. Most people who have sump pumps in the basement have occasional problems."

But how much time could Poindexter possibly have spent on the sump pump?

"There's also the water heater. The President thought Poindexter was working on that, too."

The water heater?

"Yes. If you've ever lived in an old house like this one, with aging plumbing, you know what a nuisance the water heater can be. Some mornings the President will be trying to shave, and Nancy will be yelling: 'Ron, don't use the hot water, I'm taking a shower.' Terrible way to start the day."

Yes, but what about Colonel North?

"The President was under the impression that Colonel North was in the basement doing the laundry."

I find that hard to believe.

"Why? Don't you have a washer and dryer in your basement?"

Sure.

"Well, except for good cotton shirts, it's silly to send things out to be laundered. Especially with so many permanent-press fabrics on the market today."

But there could only be so much laundry.

"True. But the President thought that Colonel North was also straightening up the tool room, the workbench, that sort of thing."

I see. The tools.

"Yes, it's incredible how they get mixed up. You go looking for a pair of pliers or a wrench and it's never where you thought you put it the last time you used it. Or sandpaper. Have you ever noticed how the sandpaper is never in the drawer where you keep the sandpaper?"

And that's what the President thought Colonel North was doing?

"That plus the traps."

What traps?

"For the mice. The President thought Colonel North was in the basement setting mouse traps. This is the worst time of year for the little rascals, when the weather turns cold. If you don't get them now, they'll soon be upstairs giving the womenfolk a terrible fright."

I see. So what you're saying is that the President didn't know that Poindexter and North were in the White House basement setting up a deal to shift the weapons payments from Iran to the anti-Sandinista contras in Nicaragua.

"No, he knew absolutely nothing about that."

What has been the President's reaction to this?

"He's damned angry."

Because they might have violated the law?

"No. Because the sump pump and water heater are still on the fritz."

●   208

Fond Memories
of '68 Convention

June 24, 1988

We're closing in on the twentieth anniversary of the 1968 Democratic convention in Chicago. That means newspapers, magazines and TV stations are going to look back and ponder the historic significance of that wild week in Chicago.

Just about everybody who was there will be telling their stories—the politicians, antiwar protesters, policemen and news people.

One former high-ranking policeman told me: "I've already been interviewed four times. And I didn't even hit anybody on the head."

We'll see flashbacks of protesters taunting cops and cops chasing protesters. We'll see Senator Abe Ribicoff scolding Mayor Daley and Daley bellowing at Ribicoff. There will be paddy wagons, tear gas, bandaged heads, the National Guard and shaggy poets chanting their mantras in Grant Park.

The long-haired Yippies, who have become short-haired yuppies, will talk about their idealistic antiwar sentiments. The retired cops will ask why idealists thought they could end a war by lobbing bags of do-do at them.

Some political historians will say that because Daley was bullheaded the convention became a riot, and that put Richard Nixon, instead of Hubert Humphrey, in the White House. And aging Chicago politicians will say that if it hadn't been for Daley, Abbie Hoffman and his dope-ridden pals would have carried off Chicago's womenfolk and eaten babies.

Me? I'll probably write something or other when the time comes. But right now, when I think about that crazy, turbulent, violent, crazy week, all I feel is nostalgia. I get so sentimental, my eyes are teary.

How can I feel sentimental and nostalgic about a week that has been described as one of the most disgraceful in Chicago's history, if not in the history of American politics?

That's easy. It was the last political convention that was fun, that wasn't carefully orchestrated and a big bore.

I'm speaking selfishly, of course. To those who had their hairy heads cracked or their political careers disrupted, it wasn't a big hoot. But, hey, every four years I have to cover these things. And given a choice between long, droning speeches or rioting in the streets, I'll take tear gas any time.

In 1972, both parties went to Miami. You try sweating out Miami in August while listening to George McGovern, a personality kid, put a nation to sleep. Or watch a thousand Republicans in white shoes gaze reverentially at Richard Nixon and Spiro Agnew.

Spend a week in New York just to watch Jimmy Carter floss his teeth. Or go all the way to Kansas City to see if Jerry Ford will stumble off the stage.

I have to admit that 1980 in Detroit had its bright side. A lot of the small-town Republicans genuinely feared that Detroit's black population might cook them in pots.

And next month we're going to Atlanta, where it will be 102 and humid, and thousands of news people will spend a week asking each other: "Do we know what Jesse wants yet?"

After that, it will be New Orleans, where it will be 105 and humid, with Republicans hoping for a miracle: George Bush stepping before the cameras to make his acceptance squeaks, but instead ripping off his coat and shirt and suddenly becoming Rambo.

If the television networks were smart, they wouldn't bother to show any of it. They'd just get out all the old film clips of 1968 in Chicago. Wouldn't you rather watch a fat cop chasing Abbie Hoffman and Jerry Rubin? Wouldn't you like to see, just one more time, Dick Gregory being lifted bodily into a paddy wagon?

Five years ago, a big California politician told me that Chicago would never get another convention because of the bitter memories of 1968. Instead, he said, they would hold the '84 convention in San Francisco because it is so civilized a city and would help the Democrats' image.

So they did. And on the first day of the convention, a big, burly guy named Erma came around the press rooms to announce that there would be an ejaculation contest that afternoon. Some image.

One of these years, they're going to wise up and come back to Chicago, where we know how to show them a good time. I'm sure we have a few canisters left over.

"Okay, World, Everybody on the Couch"

Spat Becomes
a Mass Production

March 24, 1986

I'm not going to use Norman's full name, because he has enough problems. But his story should be a lesson that in this age of heightened consciousness, we must be sensitive to the feelings of others, even if they are strangers.

Norman delivers furniture for a living. And one day he was making a delivery to a Chicago office.

He pulled his truck into the alley and began unloading. A car pulled up, and the driver, whom we will call Ron, said Norman was blocking his private parking space, which was clearly marked with a sign.

Although Norman moved his truck, Ron berated him for his discourtesy, and angry words were exchanged.

215 ●

As they quarreled, Norman noticed that Ron's speech patterns and physical movements were, to his eye, quite effeminate.

So Norman said, "Say, are you some kind of faggot?"

As Ron later put it, "When he said *that,* I saw red."

The two began wrestling, and Ron grabbed Norman's little finger and twisted it so hard that a bone broke. Then he gave Norman, who was sitting on the ground and holding his painful pinky, a few punches and went to his office, where he worked for an antique company.

After getting his finger treated, Norman called the cops and brought battery charges against Ron.

They went to court, had a trial and Ron was found guilty, even though Norman admitted that he had called Ron a faggot.

Ron paid a fine and was ordered to give Norman money for the income he lost while his finger mended.

But the dispute was far from over. Some time later, Norman made another delivery to the same alley. Ron saw him and ran out and took Norman's picture. He said he wanted it as evidence that Norman parked illegally.

Norman, saying he feared that he might get another broken finger, leaped into his truck and raced away, almost running down Ron.

Ron called the police and brought charges against Norman. Another trial was held, and this time Norman was found guilty and had to pay a fine.

But that still didn't end it. Ron was still terribly upset that Norman had called him a faggot.

"Well, he *is* gay," says Norman. "Anyone could see that. But I don't see what he's so upset about. I didn't actually call him a faggot. I just asked him if he was a faggot."

A few days ago, Ron set out to get revenge. And did he get it.

It turns out that Norman, who is married and has a

couple of kids, lives in the very heart of the city's gayest neighborhood.

This is also the neighborhood where Ron spends much of his social and recreational time.

So Ron had about a thousand handbills printed up, and he plastered the neighborhood with them, putting them under windshields and in restaurants and bars.

I'll describe the handbills.

At the top is a picture of Norman. Beneath the picture is Norman's name, address and phone number. Beneath that is this message:

THE ABOVE PERSON LIVING IN YOUR NEIGHBORHOOD REFERS TO PEOPLE AS BEING A FAGGOT.

I ASK YOU—SHOULD SUCH A PERSON BE ALLOWED TO BE A RESIDENT OF THIS COMMUNITY?

And, boy, did the community respond. Norman's phone has been ringing day and night.

"I'm getting an endless stream of obscene phone calls," says Norman. "They refer to me in all kinds of gay sexual concepts.

"And this guy [Ron] showed up outside my building and was yelling obscene things at me."

Ron justifies his handbill campaign against Norman by saying: "I wanted him to apologize for calling me a [obscenity] and for calling me a faggot."

Norm says: "I don't know what he is so excited about. I'm the one who got a broken finger."

Ron says: "He had no business calling me a faggot. He has never seen me in a compromising position or in my bedroom."

And Norman says: "The thing is, I don't have anything against gays. I have some gay friends. But he's weird."

Although Norman's phone is still ringing, and strangers are screaming strange things at him, the feud has officially ended.

The two men made their final court appearance last week, and Norman formally apologized for calling Ron a faggot. Ron accepted the apology.

But Norman still says: "I don't know why he made such a big deal out of it. If you look in the dictionary, you'll see that a faggot is just a bundle of sticks."

Proof That Bliss Is Just Ignorance

March 17, 1987

One of my fondest curbstone theories has recently been confirmed by genuine scientific research.

It has to do with why some people are chronically grouchy and depressed while others are always bubbling with enthusiasm and looking at the bright side of life.

A psychologist took a close look at students who fell into both groups. He wanted to see how they reacted when they got poor grades.

He found that those who had the gloomier outlook of life generally blamed only themselves for their subpar performances.

In contrast, those who bounce happily through life with big smiles on their faces usually found some other reason for their failings. They blamed teachers for not doing a good job or for being unfair, or they said that something had distracted them, prevented them from doing their best work. In other words, it wasn't their fault.

After analyzing the excuses of both groups, the psychologist found that those who tended to be gloomy were right—they had been at fault.

In contrast, the happiness-mongers were kidding

● 218

themselves. They, too, were at fault, but they couldn't accept it, so they found someone else to blame.

Thus, the study came to the conclusion that those who were gloomy and depressed had a far more realistic view of themselves and life in general.

But the happiness-mongers had a tendency to be unrealistic.

This is what I've always believed: Show me somebody who is always smiling, always cheerful, always optimistic, and I will show you somebody who hasn't the faintest idea what the heck is really going on.

And that most maligned creature, the chronic grouch, is depressed because he knows that there is a lot to be depressed about. He knows that every dark cloud doesn't necessarily have a silver lining. It's more likely that the cloud contains acid rain.

Slats Grobnik put it neatly when a happiness-monger once looked in his gloomy face and said: "Hey, cheer up, things always have a way of getting better."

Slats said: "If things always have a way of getting better, how come funeral parlors do so much business?"

Somebody else once told him: "After the storm, there comes the rainbow."

Slats said: "After the storm, stupid, there comes the flooded basement."

And he had an answer when another happiness-monger told him: "Remember, it's always darkest before the dawn."

Slats said: "Then how come they waited until the sun came up to bomb Pearl Harbor?"

Just look in the history books. I defy anyone to show me a picture of Abe Lincoln with a big smile on his face. He may have been the most depressed, gloom-filled man ever to hold the office of President. That's because he knew what was going on and that there was a lot to be depressed about.

219 ●

In contrast, we have Ronald Reagan, who is seldom seen without a slap-happy smile. That's because—as Reagan himself recently told us—he doesn't always know what's going on.

So we had one President who was gloomy when the most terrible weapon known to man was a short-range cannon. Now we have another who can't stop chuckling at a time when mankind has the capacity to vaporize itself.

And that should be enough to make the rest of us stop grinning.

Or try looking at the picture of the happy showbiz people who are always being shown in *People* magazine attending parties. Of course they look happy. Between the hooch and the powder they're snorting, they don't know which of their ends is up.

Contrast their facial expressions with those you see in the morning on commuter trains, buses or behind the wheels of cars. These people know exactly where they are and where they are going. They are going to work. That is reality. And that's why they're not giggling.

So I hope the above-mentioned scientific research helps put an end to the idea that people who smile a lot are in some way better than those who frown.

The scientists might even consider Slats Grobnik's theory that smiling is unnatural, that it defies nature, while frowning is a natural, since gravity pulls our faces downward.

"If nature wanted us to smile all the time," he has said, "then we would have been born with our heads upside down."

That is something to think about.

Jessica Hahn,
Top to Bottom

August 3, 1988

I don't know why anyone would be concerned about the strike by the TV writers. Even without their creative efforts, there is so much that is worthwhile on television.

For example, last night I was flipping though my cable channels, looking for a wrestling match, when suddenly I was face to face with Jessica Hahn.

I was surprised to see her because I thought that she had used up her allotment of fame and had passed on to wherever transient celebrities go. Some sort of *People* magazine graveyard, maybe buried next to little Jimmy Bakker.

But there she was, being interviewed by Larry King, so I decided to stick around and find out what she's been up to.

Because I tuned in late and missed the introduction, I didn't know why she was being interviewed.

And at that moment, she was discussing her breasts. She said that as a teen, she had been plump. So she dieted and lost forty pounds. But this left her with unusual proportions. She said her breasts drooped almost to her knees.

I thought that King would surely ask her about the difficulty of buying suitable undergarments. Or suggest that maybe a couple of old inner tubes would do the job.

But they went on to discuss her body. Apparently, she has gone to a California body shop—the kind for people, not cars—and had her body rebuilt. New nose, teeth and anything that was hanging too low.

Then it became clear why they were talking about such highly personal matters. I mean, if I had breasts or

221

anything else that hung down to my knees, I would not go on Larry King's show and talk about it.

But it turned out that Ms. Hahn is displaying her rebuilt body in *Playboy* magazine. As you may recall, last year she displayed her unaltered body. So we will have a chance to compare the old and rebuilt bodies and marvel at the wonders of modern science.

I was about to switch to the public broadcasting channel, for their nightly installment on the sex life of insects, when King said he was going to take calls from the live audience.

Sensing the potential for conflict, I stayed tuned. And I was right. The first caller was a lady from the South, and she didn't care for Ms. Hahn's morals one danged bit.

She demanded to know how Ms. Hahn could be a good Christian and flaunt her body so shamelessly.

I didn't take notes, but Ms. Hahn said something to the effect that the good Lord, in his infinite wisdom, had given her this opportunity, so she took it, and still considered herself a good girl.

The caller didn't agree. She thought that the good Lord would disapprove of Ms. Hahn's conduct, and that she was a bad girl.

Although I'm not a theologian, debates of this kind fascinate me. But it seems to me that Ms. Hahn was probably right. If the Lord didn't want Ms. Hahn posing for *Playboy,* He could have prevented it. All He'd have to do is make her body grow fur. I mean, you never see a yak in the centerfold.

Several other callers spoke and a clear pattern developed. Most of the women disapproved of Ms. Hahn showing her new breasts in a magazine. But most of the men said they thought it was just fine. I guess it means that men are just more liberal.

Then, to the amazement of King, Ms. Hahn and me, a call came from Hugh Hefner's fiancée, a young lady named Kimberly Conrad. I don't believe that's her real name. My guess is that she was born Thelma Fugelblatt, but Hefner doesn't carry on with girls named Thelma.

Anyway, Kimberly and Jessica are pals, since Jessica lives in the Hefner playhouse, and they told each other what beautiful people and wonderful human beings they were. It brought a tear to my eye. Or maybe I'm developing a sty.

Then Hefner himself came on the phone. He giggled. I've known him, on and off, mostly off, for about twenty-five years, and every time I've heard him talk, he giggles. I suppose that if I had led his life, I'd giggle, too. If I had any strength left.

He, too, said that Jessica was a wonderful human being. And she said he was a beautiful person. I don't recall if she said Hefner was a wonderful human being, but I'm sure she thinks so.

There was more, but I had to walk out of the room and pull my emotions together, I was so choked up.

As the program ended, Larry King asked Jessica what she was going to do with the rest of her life. She thought for a moment, then said that she was going to write a book.

At least I think that's what she said. A plane went over just as she was responding, so I didn't hear her too clearly.

So it's possible that she said she was going to read one.

Rambo's Hitch
with the Coeds

July 4, 1985

Here it is, the Fourth of July, and America has a new hero, a symbol of patriotism and bravery.

Who? Rambo, of course.

Rambo is the fearsome Vietnam vet created and played by Sylvester Stallone who has gone back to Vietnam to look for American prisoners.

As a one-man army, filling the theater screen with bullets and dead Asiatics, Rambo fights the war again. And this time we win.

It's a fantasy, of course, but many people are taking it seriously. Some peace-mongers fear that it is a right-wing message that we should go into Central America and kick butts.

On the other hand, some shrinks say it may have therapeutic value. But then, some shrinks can find therapeutic value in a case of hay fever.

Among those taking Rambo most seriously is Stallone himself. He has gone on TV to talk about how the movie is his effort to give the veterans of that war some credit for what they did.

As he said in one interview: "The people who pushed the wrong button all took a powder. The vets got the raw deal and were left holding the bag. What *Rambo* is saying is that if they could fight again, it would be different."

Well, I hate to mention this, but speaking of taking a powder . . .

After hearing Stallone, I became curious about how he spent those years when members of his generation, with whom he now identifies so closely, were getting the raw deal.

● 224

It turns out that Stallone, who was born in 1946 and was reared in a prosperous family, sought higher education during the Vietnam War.

And he went pretty high to get it—3,300 feet up the Alps to the American College of Switzerland.

Having been a teenage weight lifter (his mother owned a gymnasium), his bulging biceps led him to part-time chores at the college. As he described it in another interview:

"Part of the deal was that I would teach physical education to a lot of wealthy American girls.

"The first thing I learned was that rich girls do not jump or sweat. All of them got A's just for showing up.

"I was also supposed to be a kind of chaperon, assuring that no lustful positions would be assumed while I was on duty. I was to protect the girls from the hordes of mountain climbers, the pillaging hunters who kept trying to woo them off to their cabins, those lotharios in lederhosen who came swinging through the windows of the dorm on ropes and absconding into the woods with damsels in distress. Let's just say I failed at my job.

"One of my friends at school was Prince Paul of Ethiopia. He was having trouble with the other boys, and I helped him out. He felt indebted to me, so he bought me about thirty wristwatches and lent me five hundred francs, enough to start up a clandestine hamburger joint.

"They didn't have beef as we know beef, so I made a mixture of veal and horsemeat and called it a Stallone lumpburger. . . . The girls in the dorm loved it. I used to send up tons of it every night, and it would be smuggled from room to room."

The frisky madcap later left Switzerland, the girls and his pal the prince and switched to the University of Miami as a drama major.

Then it was off to an acting career in New York,

225 ●

where he landed some nude roles off Broadway. And the rest is movie history.

So, during the years when he could have been a real-life Rambo, the strapping Stallone was in Switzerland, teaching rich girls how to touch their toes, and in Miami, improving his tan.

Now Rambo, having won in Vietnam, is going to return in another burst of glory and gunfire in some other troubled part of the world—*Rambo III,* coming soon to your local theaters.

As Stallone says, "Rambo is a war machine that can't be turned off."

Well, better late than never, I guess.

Getting a Piece of the Wreck

October 7, 1985

One of these days, Tommy is going to be a success. Right now he's only a flunky messenger at a Chicago law firm. But he's going to rise above that because he has that rare quality: He knows an opportunity when he sees it.

Such as the other morning. Tommy happened to be nearby when a city bus and a truck collided. Nobody was killed, but about eighteen passengers were banged up.

What did Tommy do? Did he stand there on the curb and gawk, the way most people do when they see an accident? Or just shrug and go about his business?

You bet he didn't. Tommy went into action.

No, he didn't rush aboard and try to rescue someone

or anything like that. The firemen were already there, taking care of the injured.

What Tommy did was to slip into the bus through the side door, flop into a seat and begin groaning as if in excruciating pain.

"We saw him," one of the amused firemen said later. "He came sneaking in the back while we were taking people off through the front door. He was a pretty good actor, too."

Although they knew he was faking, the firemen treated him as if he were really injured. Tommy moaned and groaned all the way to the hospital.

The doctors gave him some pain pills, and Tommy took the rest of the day off from work and went home to rest and, presumably, ponder the size of his personal injury lawsuit.

When we phoned and told him that the firemen had seen him creeping aboard the bus, he just said:

"Hmmm. It must have been somebody else."

Well, that's possible. As any cop or fireman will tell you, at any big accident involving public transportation, the injury list just keeps growing.

"I remember when I was at a train crash a few years ago," a policeman told me. "There were dozens of people jumping from the other platform, trying to get into the wrecked train. I mean, dozens of people trying to get in there. It was an amazing sight.

"Another time, I saw a cab get rear-ended with a couple of little old ladies in it. These ladies were just sitting there waiting for the police to come and make out a report, and then these guys who had been on the sidewalk and saw the accident jumped into the cab and starting holding their necks and moaning. They almost pushed the old ladies out into the street."

A fireman recalled an accident on an elevated train.

227

"We had a ladder that was kind of hard to maneuver, and I was trying to get it up. There were a few spectators standing there on the sidewalk, and I asked them to give me a hand with it.

"So a few of the guys give me a hand and I climb up and I go in the train, helping some of the people out.

"I'm up there a little while, and I see this guy stretched out over the seat like he's close to death. And it's one of the guys who helped me put up the ladder.

"I told him, 'Hey, clown, get out of here.' He gets up and walks out. But he says to me: 'You'll hear from my attorney.'"

But for initiative, you can't beat the crowd that was in a scruffy tavern the day a car slammed into a bus right in front of the place.

A bus supervisor who was there said: "You never saw a tavern clear out like that. They were coming out in droves and trying to get on the bus or lying down in the street. One minute they were all inside, sitting on bar stools and drinking. The next minute they were outside, flat on their backs, holding their necks and yelling 'Whiplash, I got whiplash.'

"Another time I arrived at the scene of an elevated accident and I couldn't believe what I was seeing. People were actually shinnying up the el structure to get in on the accident. They could have broken their necks to fake a broken neck."

Is it worth the effort? Well, somewhere out there is a guy I knew years ago when he was having trouble making the rent. I'm told he is now a millionaire.

I was sure he'd do okay the day he showed up wearing a neck brace. He said he'd been sitting in his car, waiting for the light to change, when he glanced in his rear-view mirror and saw a couple in the Cadillac behind him having a quarrel.

He also saw that the car was creeping forward, but the driver, distracted by his conversation, wasn't paying attention.

When the Caddy's bumper touched his bumper, he was ready. His door snapped open and he went flying into the street, writhing in agony.

He phoned his brother-in-law, an attorney, from the emergency room and the lawsuit was filed within the week.

I don't know if that started him on his road to financial success.

But it was an early indication that he had—what shall we call it—the right stuff, Chicago style.

Nobody Ever Got Raped by a Book

June 11, 1986

When I was a young crime reporter, I hung around police stations and watched the dregs drift by.

They included every sort of sexual adventurer. Rapists, peepers, flashers, child molesters, zoo invaders and guys who wore pink negligees.

Some were harmless; others were deadly. But one thing that I never saw was a dirty book sticking out of any of their pockets.

Nor did any of them confess to having dashed from a porno movie house to satisfy their lusts.

That would have been unlikely, because there was little pornography available. There were no smutty bookstores or porno movie houses. If you wanted to read something lewd, you were limited to the old eight-pagers—silly little cartoon pamphlets that showed Mickey Mouse doing it to Minnie.

For a dirty movie, you had to know somebody who could get you into an American Legion post where they were showing a stag film starring some skinny guy wearing black socks and a pimply woman who moved like she had just worked a double shift on an assembly line.

Yet sex crimes were a routine entry on the police blotter. Anything that sex offenders do today, they were doing then.

But now we're being told by some Washington panel that pornography is a major cause of sexual violence. Convenience store chains have been pressured into not selling magazines that have centerfolds. And in many states and local communities, there is a new push for more restrictive laws.

So my question is, if pornography turns people into sex fiends, why did we have so much sexual violence before the stuff was available?

One group of experts say that because of pornography, there is more sexual violence than there used to be.

But another group will say that's bunk, that the increase in the crime statistics is simply the result of victims reporting crimes that they used to keep quiet out of embarrassment or because cops and prosecutors brushed them off.

Child abuse, for example. Incest. People used to be ashamed to go to the law. Now most aren't.

So nobody has made a conclusive case that Hefner and Guccione are guilty of anything more provocative than being a couple of pompous, profiteering jerks. Or that seeing an X-rated movie inspires a lout to dash into the streets and drag a woman into a gangway.

But for the sake of argument, let's conclude that pornography does inspire a certain amount of violence.

If that's the case, we should be consistent in outlawing things that cause violence.

Consider that in recent years, there have been more than 220 bombings of abortion clinics. Bombs are pretty violent devices.

And what motivates the bombers? Those who have been arrested have expressed deep religious convictions. They say their beliefs justified setting off bombs.

Then there have been the extremist groups that shoot rural sheriffs, talk show hosts and lawyers they suspect of being liberal. They, too, spout religious devotion.

So maybe we should begin considering the outlawing of religion because it is the root cause of so much violence.

But you, as a religious person, answer that religion isn't the cause, that people who set off bombs or shoot talk show hosts have a few screws loose and will always find a reason to be violent.

I agree. Just as I agree with those who say that the guy who crawls through a window and rapes and murders a woman or a child didn't get turned on by some $6 paperback he bought in Times Square.

Maybe he did it because his brain cells aren't arranged right, or he was dropped on his head as a kid or he is simply evil. And there have been people like that long before the first book was printed.

Personally, I don't like pornography. But not because I fear it will turn me or someone else into a raging fiend. I dislike it because it is tasteless, embarrassing and boring.

But that's no reason to ban it. If being tasteless or embarrassing or boring was a crime, we'd have to get rid

231 ●

of 90 percent of the TV shows and hit records, close down most of the franchise food joints, muzzle the politicians and prohibit any preacher from talking more than 90 seconds.

Ah, those are some censorship movements I might like to join.

Surprise!
It's the Avon Lady

September 7, 1984

At one time or another, most of us have heard the doorbell ring and a female voice say "Avon calling."

But I doubt if we've heard it quite the way a young man named Eddie O'Brien recently did.

Let me start at the beginning.

O'Brien, eighteen, has a kid sister, Lisa, fifteen, and Lisa had a part-time job selling Avon cosmetics.

One day, Lisa's supervisor phoned to ask about Lisa's sales. Lisa hadn't been selling much; so the supervisor said she would come over with some sales instruction books. They made an appointment to meet the next morning at the O'Brien home.

The next day, Lisa waited, but the morning passed without the Avon supervisor appearing.

Lisa had a baby-sitting job that afternoon, so she finally hopped on her bike and left for it.

Eddie was home at the time, but he didn't know anything about Lisa's appointment with the Avon supervisor.

A little while after Lisa left, the Avon lady showed up. She rang the doorbell, but nobody answered.

● 232

That's because Eddie had gone into the bathroom to take a shower.

Seeing that the door was unlocked, the Avon lady let herself into the house.

This was a mistake because the O'Briens have a dog. Although it is a small dog, a terrier, it has a fierce nature and sharp teeth.

So as the Avon lady walked through the house, looking for Lisa, the dog darted out from under a table, leaped into the air and nipped the Avon lady on her bottom.

Naturally, this made her scream. It also caused her to try to escape from the dog.

Seeing a door slightly open, she ran to it, rushed into the room and closed the door behind her.

It turned out to be the downstairs bathroom. And in it, behind sliding shower doors, was young Eddie.

Because of the noise of the shower and his own singing, and because the bathroom door had been almost closed, Eddie had been unaware of the presence of the Avon lady and her encounter with his dog.

All he knew was that the bathroom door had suddenly opened and closed and through the glass he could see the silhouette of another human being.

It scared the hell out of him.

And that's understandable. When you think about it, there are few moments when we are as totally vulnerable and defenseless as when we are standing bare-bottomed naked in the shower. Maybe Anthony Perkins, in the movie *Psycho,* planted the seeds of fear deep in our subconscious.

Eddie opened the shower door an inch or two and peered out.

There, in his bathroom, stood a total stranger. True, the stranger was a woman. But who says women can't be homicidal maniacs or fiends?

So Eddie screamed: "Who are you?"

"I'm the Avon lady," she said.

Now, what would you think upon hearing those words under those circumstances? Right. You would think that you were dealing with a complete loony. Which is exactly what Eddie thought.

"Avon lady?" Eddie screamed. "Avon lady? What are you doing in my bathroom?"

"I was just bitten by your dog."

"My dog bit you?"

"Yes, I'm hiding from your dog."

"I don't understand any of this," Eddie said.

The woman explained and the thumping of Eddie's heart subsided enough for him to say: "What do you want me to do?"

"Do something about your dog."

"But I don't have any clothes in here."

That problem was solved when she handed him a towel.

"Turn around," Eddie said.

In a few minutes, Eddie had corralled the raging little beast in the kitchen and the Avon lady was on her way to seek medical treatment for her wounded bottom.

Since then, Lisa has given up her Avon job. And the Avon lady had a lawyer send the O'Brien family a letter, asking them to pay for the medical treatment.

"The letter said that our dog caused her great bodily injury," said Eddie's mother, Maria.

"Well, I don't know about that," Maria said. "But I'll tell you one thing. She didn't do much good for Eddie's nerves."

● 234

After the Heroics, Hustlers Take Over

March 25, 1988

How about this as a plot for a thriller TV movie?

There's this sweet little girl, only eighteen months old, playing outside her home in a Texas town.

Suddenly, terror. She falls into a hole. It is a deep and narrow abandoned well.

She's alive. The challenge is to get her out of the well, which is not much wider than a drainpipe. There's no way an adult can squeeze in and get to her. And if they try to widen it by digging, she will be smothered.

The rescuers work out a plan and go to work. For three days, they frantically drill another shaft next to the one the girl is in.

Reporters and TV crews flock to the scene. The whole country watches and waits, filled with dread. Will they reach her in time? Will she live or die?

At last, the second shaft is finished, and they tunnel to her and bring her up. She is cold and injured, but alive.

Her parents rejoice. The rescuers hug each other. Much of the nation weeps.

Sounds familiar? Of course. It's the dramatic true story of baby Jessica McClure, who held the attention of the whole country in 1987.

And the dramatic story goes on, but in a different way.

In a fascinating account this week, the *New York Times* described how the Jessica story has evolved into something tacky.

The movie people have swooped down on Midland, Texas, with their contracts, deals, money offers and proposed scripts.

235 ●

They're competing to buy the rights to the story from those who lived the story, the rescuers and Jessica's parents.

And human nature being what it is, the rescuers are now fighting among themselves.

They've split into two groups. One is made up of the official rescuers: the police, firefighters and other public employees. The other group is made up of the volunteers.

Each group is claiming to have the rights to the story. Each group has hired lawyers. And each group is accusing the other of greed while claiming only pure motives for itself.

The Hollywood people are, of course, acting as they always do. Which means that compared to them, a used car dealer is a living saint.

Some want to spice up the story by making the marriage of Jessica's parents shaky. Then, of course, the child's peril and rescue bring them back together, get it?

Others want to create one heroic figure among the 400 people who took part in the rescue. Got to have a star, right?

And while the Hollywood hustlers are making their pitch, the two competing rescue groups are squabbling over who gets what if a deal is made.

Having dealt with Hollywood dealmakers, I know how sleazy they can be. And I also know how lacking in creativity most of them are. Consider what they produce. Without car crashes, naked bodies, blood squirting from several heads and everybody saying "Shit," nine out of ten movies wouldn't be made.

So I'm not surprised that they've overlooked a far superior movie plot than the one they've been chasing in Texas.

Let's face it, we all know what happened to little Jessica. That means we all know how a movie about her will end. Do we want to sit through almost two hours of guys digging a shaft when we know the outcome?

Not me. But here's a plot that would be a grabber.

The movie opens with a little girl playing in her yard in a Texas town. She falls into an old narrow well. She's trapped. The rescuers frantically dig a parallel shaft. They tunnel to her and bring her up—cold, injured, but alive. Her parents rejoice, everybody hugs and the nation weeps and sighs with relief.

Right. Same plot. But we do all that in the first fifteen or twenty minutes, which is really all it takes to tell that part of the story.

Then the rest of the movie develops. In come the Hollywood hustlers with their contracts, their deals, their big money offers.

And we watch as greed sets in, envy and distrust. All those good old boy rescuers are suddenly in warring camps. Pals who hugged are now ready to duke it out. Everybody is saying: "Where's mine? How big is the pie? Is there enough for everybody?"

The Hollywood hustlers are tripping over one another trying to nail down a deal. And deals are made—but quickly unmade when somebody's agent says they ought to have a bigger piece of the action.

Every so often, we can cut to Jessica's parents warily peering through their curtains at the dealmakers camped in the front yard while Jessica asks: "When can I go out and play again?"

How would my script end? I have the perfect closer.

One of the dealmakers finally gets the names of the rescuers he needs on a contract. Then he persuades Jessica's folks to sign.

He rushes from Jessica's house, triumphantly waving the contract over his head.

And he falls in an old well.

Trust me, it'll work. Everybody loves a happy ending.

Adding Insult
to a Tragedy

June 26, 1985

After a tragedy, somebody has to pick up the pieces. Funeral arrangements. Legal documents. Personal effects. These things have to be taken care of.

So on June 14, Oscar Smith got in his tow truck and went to get his dead stepson's car.

His stepson, Dimitric Grant, eighteen, had been killed. It was another of those stupid, pointless deaths that happen so often on the city streets.

Grant was just sitting in his car. A gang member shot him, though Grant wasn't involved in gangs. Just the opposite: He worked regularly and coached a Little League team.

When Smith, in his truck, got to the car, the detectives were still there. They told him he couldn't have it yet. They had to examine it for evidence: fingerprints, ballistics and such.

They said they'd need it for about five days. Then he could take it away.

The five days passed. The funeral was held, the family and friends wept and prayed, and the young man was buried.

Then Smith called the Police Department and asked whether he could come and get the car. Somebody told him to call the police auto pound, which is where cars are towed.

He called the pound.

"The fella on the phone, he says that, yeah, the car is there and I can come and get it and it'll cost me $80.

"I asked him what the $80 was for. He says that was $50 for towing and $5 a day for six days of storage.

"I told him what happened, that our boy had been murdered and that I had come for the car but that they told me they had to keep it for evidence.

"But he says to me, 'That'll be $80 if you want the car.'

"Now, isn't that something? He gets murdered, and now we have to pay them $80 to get his car back. It's almost like paying a tax for being murdered."

That did seem peculiar. It's one thing for a car to be abandoned on the street and towed in as a nuisance.

But young Grant didn't abandon his car. He happened to die in it. And his stepfather had been willing to tow it away.

Nor does the word storage seem appropriate for an object that was being studied for evidence in a crime. If a murder had been committed in somebody's kitchen, and they wanted to study a coffeepot for fingerprints, would the victim's family have to pay a storage fee for the coffeepot?

We called the police department to find out why Smith had to pay a fee. The answer varied, depending on who we talked to.

One man said he might not have to pay the fee. Another said he might have to pay for the tow but not for the storage. Another said he would have to pay the whole thing. And somebody else said he wasn't sure whether Smith could have the car at all, because they weren't sure who the car belonged to now that young Grant was dead.

Meanwhile, another day passed. And when Smith called again, he was told that, yes, he could come and get the car but the fee had gone up to $85. Another day, another $5.

"But at least they said I could come and take the car," Smith said. "But they said that I should be sure and bring the death certificate with me."

Since they had arrested somebody in the killing, you

239 ●

would think that they wouldn't need a document to tell them that Grant was indeed dead.

But Smith got the death certificate and put $85 in his wallet and went to get the car.

A little later he phoned and said: "I got here, but I can't have the car yet. They said that there was a hold put on it by some detectives. They want to keep it for evidence for a while.

"I don't know how long that's gonna be. But I guess it'll keep costing me $5 a day."

Smith then said: "I got to get away from all this. I'm going up north and go fishing for a while. I have to get all these things off my mind."

He'd better not stay away fishing too long. Those murder taxes can start mounting up.

Flighty Lawsuit Has
Lousy Karma

September 13, 1985

I've always enjoyed the language used by lawyers in lawsuits to describe the agonies of their clients.

Even in a minor mishap, nobody suffers moderate discomfort, a mild upset, a queazy stomach or a slight headache.

It's always excruciating emotional or physical distress, permanent and debilitating suffering, painful aches and other cruel miseries.

And you don't even have to have a skinned knee to feel that way. An insensitive husband, as described in a divorce suit, can cause pains that would have made a Spanish Inquisitor envious.

● 240

So I was fascinated by a lawsuit filed in the state of Washington by seven people who have accused a famous guru of failing to teach them how to fly.

The seven filed their suit against the Maharishi Mahesh Yogi, who is one of the bigger-named gurus around because he used to teach transcendental meditation to the Beatles, Mia Farrow and other stars. He even has appeared on *Merv Griffin* a few times to chant a mantra and smile benignly, which all successful gurus must do.

From what the suit said, the guru was supposed to teach the seven how to fly. Not on airplanes, of course, because you don't need a guru to do that. Only a credit card.

Apparently, the guru was supposed to teach them how to rise off the floor and float around. The suit didn't say if they expected to do loops and dives, spins or any other tricky maneuvers.

Nor did the suit say why they wanted to fly. To soar above rush-hour traffic? Amaze their friends at parties? Get a better view at sporting events?

But the fact is, they did not learn to fly, though they tried.

It seems that the guru's flying lessons consisted of having them assume the now-famous lotus position, which is favored by many gurus and is a useful position to know if you don't want to spend a lot of money on furniture.

Once in the lotus position, they were supposed to concentrate and meditate and bounce. The bouncing was supposed to eventually get them airborne.

But, as they discovered, all that happened was that the bouncing hurt their legs and they never got more than an inch or so off the ground.

I suppose that is a form of flying, but I doubt if a few one- or two-inch bounces from the lotus position would get anybody an invitation to perform at a country fair.

241

So now they want $9 million in damages from the guru to compensate them for the disappointment and suffering they experienced in not learning to fly.

Their suffering included "negative emotional, psychological and physical effects."

All that bouncing, trying to get into a decent flight pattern, caused "severe and continuing pain" in their bones.

And the shock and despair of discovering that they *couldn't fly* "arrested and retarded the normal process of maturation and development."

That sounds like a lot of misery just from assuming a lotus position and doing a little bouncing. But then, I've never tried it, because I have a morbid fear of flying.

I was unable to talk to the seven suffering nonfliers because they used the phony names of John and Jane Doe in their lawsuit. I don't blame them. Besides all the other physical and emotional trauma they suffered, they'd probably take a certain amount of needling at the office.

But I called the office of the lawyer who filed the suit and found that three of the seven would-be Johnny Seagulls had registered at a school run by the guru, where people are taught to squat, chant and get all groovy and cuddly with the universe.

"And the contract they had wasn't fulfilled," a spokesman said. "Physically flying is what they guaranteed, and they would reach this through hours and hours of meditation. We even have videotapes of it. It is really weird."

He wouldn't give us the names of the seven because they fear that making their names public may subject them to revenge by the guru's followers. I suppose that's a wise precaution. They might slip them a bad mantra.

Anyway, I for one am glad that they didn't learn to fly. If they could do it, who knows how many others might develop the skill?

● 242

And who would want flocks of people soaring above? We've already got enough disgusting problems with pigeons.

Fear of Flying
Isn't Groundless

April 17, 1984

The moment I saw that *Newsweek* magazine's cover story was about phobias, I thumbed through looking for the part about mine.

I skimmed past the part about the agoraphobic (fear of spaces) lady who had come out of her apartment only three times in sixty-one years. And the gephyrophobic (bridges) man whose wife puts him in the car trunk when they cross a dreaded span. And all the other examples of phobics who fear snakes, shopping malls, strangers, eating in public, dogs, germs, vehicles or darkness.

Then I found it. Aerophobia: the fear of flying. My own, personal phobia.

As I've probably mentioned before, I have this thing about airplanes. I've been on a plane only once in the past twenty-five years. Actually, I've been on two, but I don't count the second one because I scrambled off before the stewardess closed the door.

Since I won't fly, naturally I'm interested in the subject of not flying, and I read all the articles about it—especially those that suggest a remedy.

Just once, I'd like to read something that got it right. And, I'm sorry to say, the current *Newsweek* article didn't succeed.

It said: "The fear of flying is usually experienced as

243

the fear of being trapped inside an airplane. It is a kind of claustrophobia of the soul that has very little to do with the real dangers of air travel."

What nonsense. It has nothing to do with being trapped inside an airplane. Or any "claustrophobia of the soul," whatever that means.

I don't mind at all being trapped inside an airplane. I could get on a plane right now, sit down and be totally relaxed, comfortable, without a trace of fear. *As long as the thing stayed on the ground, where it belongs.*

That's the part that bothers me—not being inside that tin tube. But being inside of it when it is hurtling through the air at the speed of a bullet, four or five miles above the nearest rooftop.

Over the years, I've tried to explain that to those who urge me to fly or try to get to the root of my resistance.

I tried going to a shrink. He spent hours listening to me talk about all the things that can happen to an airplane. Birds flying into the jet intake. Mechanics with hangovers forgetting to tighten bolts. Guys in the control tower having nervous breakdowns or sniffing glue. Pilots with suicidal tendencies. Some passenger jumping up and saying: "Take me to Havana or we go boom!"

When I finished our last session, nothing had changed, except the psychiatrist had become so scared that he wouldn't fly either. And after all I did for him, he still sent me a bill.

Once an airline sent a public relations man over with a briefcase full of statistics that were meant to be reassuring.

He said things like: "You know, the chances of your being killed while crossing the street are much greater than of being killed in a plane."

I said: "Yeah? When I cross the street, I look both ways first. If I look both ways on an airplane, will that prevent the pilot from running into the side of a mountain?"

He said: "Do you realize that there are more dangers of being killed or injured in an accident in your own home than on an airplane?"

I said: "Yeah? Well, I've never landed my home in a swamp at two hundred miles an hour."

He said: "You are in far more danger while driving your car."

I said: "When I get ice on *my* windshield, I stop and scrape it off. Can your pilot do *that*?"

When I finished with him, he wouldn't ride an escalator.

But to get back to the *Newsweek* article. It provided possible cures, but they were the usual ones, such as the group therapy sessions run by the airlines during which they teach you how to relax and tell you how safe airplanes are.

A pilot who runs one of the programs described the fear this way: "When people go on an airplane journey, it's very similar to the journey of life."

More nonsense. I don't journey through my life at 650 miles an hour, 26,000 feet above the wilderness of Ohio, with my stomach in my mouth.

That public relations man tried to get me to join such a class. I asked him: "Do a lot of people do that?" He said: "Oh, sure. You know, there are millions of people who feel the way you do." I said: "They can't all be wrong."

I've tried all the remedies. The only one that worked was when a friend in Washington, upon hearing that I was taking a train back to Chicago, suggested that I drink martinis until I was ready to ride an airplane. It worked. After only nine large martinis, I rode the plane. The only trouble is, after nine martinis I'd also be willing to ride a bull or a python.

I even tried hypnotism once, but I don't think the hypnotist was very good. I told him that I wanted hypnotism to help me fly. When he put me under, I flapped my arms and quacked like a duck.

So I've given up. And maybe it is not a bad idea. According to the *Newsweek* article, Ronald Reagan didn't launch his political career until he overcame his dread of flying. That means that if he hadn't overcome it, he wouldn't be President today.

Who says phobias are bad?

Nature Not Tame Enough for Town

September 27, 1984

Basically, there are two kinds of homeowners: Those who are fanatics about cutting and trimming their lawns, and those who don't give a damn.

When I had a lawn, I fell into the second category. It was cut if a neighborhood kid with a mower wanted to earn a few bucks. If not, it grew.

It wasn't that I was lazy, although I am. But I've never thought that a closely cropped lawn looked any better than a shaggy one. In fact, I've always thought weeds looked just as good as grass.

One of my neighbors used to complain bitterly that my free-spirit lawn was destroying real estate values on the block. But she shut up after I threatened to decorate my shaggy lawn with a couple of spare tires, an old Cadillac fender and some empty muscatel bottles.

This is why I've become a distant admirer of Stephen

Kenney, who lives in Kenmore, New York, a suburb of Buffalo.

Kenney recently stood trial and was found guilty of failing to cut his weedy and wildflower-filled lawn. There may be other people who have been taken into court for failing to cut a lawn, but Kenney is the first I've heard about.

Kenney, thirty, is not lazy. He is a nature lover and an admirer of Henry David Thoreau, the nineteenth-century naturalist. Kenney says: "I refuse to mow my lawn because it is an environmentally unsound practice and against my most basic principles."

Unfortunately, not all of Kenney's neighbors share these principles. So when they saw the daisies and poppies and other wildflowers mingling with chest-high grass on his small lawn, some of them complained.

To explain to them why he didn't cut his lawn, Kenney put a sign up that said:

"Notice to all concerned. This lawn is not an example of sloth. It is a natural yard growing the way God intended. It does not attract mosquitoes or other pests. The plants planted here do not emit noxious fumes. And no valuable natural resources like water or gas are wasted on this environment."

One of his neighbors responded with a letter, saying Kenney was "dangerous" and a "subversive." And he squealed to village officials.

Somebody looked in the local law book and decided that Kenney was violating an ordinance that requires people to maintain their property so as to "assure the desirable residential character of the property."

The ordinances also require that lawns be "clean and free of physical hazards" and that "undergrowth and accumulation of plant life be controlled."

Village inspectors went out to see Kenney and told

247

him to cut his lawn or face legal action.

"Never," he said.

So Kenney was hauled into court, where some of his neighbors testified.

Several said they didn't mind the miniforest. In fact, they thought the wildflowers looked kind of nice.

But others said they found it "offensive." And they feared it would provide a hiding place for field mice.

One horrified woman even said: "I saw a mouse come out of there and run along the driveway to the backyard."

The judge wound up agreeing with the complainers. In his judicial wisdom, he pointed out that even naturalist Thoreau had to impose certain controls over nature at Walden Pond, such as bumping off a woodchuck that kept raiding his bean patch.

And he found Kenney guilty and told him he would have to pay a fine of $50 a day as long as the lawn was unmowed.

Disgusted, Kenney, a graduate student, said: "I don't think it's anyone's business whether I cut it or not. And it's not really a lawn. It's a wildflower meadow. You don't cut down flowers just because some of your neighbors complain. It is asinine, completely asinine."

Kenney says he is going to appeal the lawn-cutting ruling. And, until the appeal is exhausted, he says: "I ain't paying and I ain't cutting."

Incidentally, curiosity prompted me to call the village's housing inspector and ask him this question:

"Under your lawn ordinance, could a person get rid of his grass and replace it with one of those plastic, artificial lawns? You know, the kind that they have in some baseball stadiums."

Without hesitating, he said: "Oh, sure. It would be legal."

● 248

Plastic is okay, but wildflowers aren't.
The world gets nuttier and nuttier.

Hard to Face Up to
Pie Prank Now

April 11, 1985

I thought the pie-in-the-face fad was long and gratefully dead. You probably remember—about twelve years ago pies were flying everywhere. People went into the prankster business, calling themselves Pie in the Eye, Inc. or Pie in the Face Ltd., and charging $50 or $100 to hit somebody with a cream pie.

Some disgruntled victims filed lawsuits. One woman collected $5,000 because being hit by a pie made her so nervous she had to start seeing a psychiatrist. So the craze faded away. But not completely.

In Connecticut, a judge is trying to make sense out of a recent pie-throwing incident.

It seems that a woman was angry because a junior high school principal had been strict with her daughter.

She hired a guy to hit the principal with a pie during a graduation ceremony. The principal, not amused, had the guy pinched.

The woman, fearing exposure, allegedly offered the pie thrower a bribe to conceal her identity. And she allegedly offered a relative a bribe to take the blame.

This has led her to being charged with breach of the peace, tampering with a witness and bribery.

I could have told the woman not to mess around with pie throwing. I tried it once and it involved me in one of

249

the most embarrassing episodes in an already shameful career.

When the pie fad began, I was writing for the *Chicago Daily News,* and on a slow news day I asked the readers which well-known Chicagoans they thought should be hit in the face with a pie.

They responded by the thousands, suggesting dozens of celebrities, including politicians, athletes, actors, actresses, broadcasters and disc jockeys.

But the most votes were for a TV weatherman, known at the time for his boisterous behavior on camera.

So I hired a guy who had just gone into the pie-tossing business to carry out the readers' wishes.

After finishing his evening broadcast, the TV weatherman came out of his studio on State Street, strolling along with his fellow anchormen.

Up stepped the pie man, who gave him a cheerful hello and shoved the whipped-cream mess into his face.

A photographer, who had been lurking nearby, recorded the scene for history, and the next day it was in the paper.

This led to two immediate developments:

First, my phone screamed and my mailbox overflowed with the reactions of civilized people who said I was an idiot, a boor and an adolescent.

I couldn't argue with them. Having somebody hit in the face with a pie sure wasn't an example of subtle British wit.

But it became worse. A couple of days after the pie was thrown, another newspaper came out with a story on page one, gleefully raising questions about the character of the pie thrower I had hired.

To the pie thrower's embarrassment, and my amazement, the story disclosed that he was an ex-convict and a confidence man who did creative things with credit cards.

●   250

So there I was, in the public's perception, plotting and collaborating with a shady character to carry out an assault on a nice, jovial weatherman.

People called to accuse me of being everything from a puppy thief to a schoolyard flasher.

And it got even worse.

The disclosures about his past caused the pie thrower to lose his regular job. And he blamed me for his troubles, which was somewhat unfair, because I hadn't told him to moonlight as a pie thrower.

He was so upset that he threatened to sue me. But after thinking about it, he realized that he wouldn't have much of a case.

So he threatened to bump me off, although I assured him that, given a choice, I'd rather be sued.

After a while, he calmed down, so did the publicity, and the whole silly thing faded away.

But for a long time, many people, including my friends, would ask me, "How could you do something that stupid?"

And I've never been able to come up with an explanation except the one given by a guy who took off all of his clothes and jumped into a cactus patch.

When asked why he did it, he said, "Well, it seemed like a good idea at the time."

Harvard Art Class
Has a Bone to Pick

November 13, 1987

I hesitate to comment on contemporary art because when I've done it in the past, art experts have called me

251 ●

a boor and a philistine, which hurt my feelings.

For example, I once became curious about an art exhibit at a Chicago gallery. It consisted of the artist lying motionless between sheets of glass for several days. By doing this, he became the art object.

It created considerable enthusiasm among art lovers. But what interested me was how the artist could remain in that position for so long without going to the men's room, and I asked the gallery about it.

They told me that it wasn't relevant to the artistic message he was conveying, which I didn't understand either.

I finally got them to admit that the artist solved the problem I asked about by just wetting his pants. When I reported this, the art community said I was crude and insensitive.

They were probably right, but at least my pants were dry.

Now I've come across another contemporary art story, which I've been trying to understand.

An art lecturer at Harvard has assigned her students to make sculptures from chicken bones.

This, in itself, isn't unusual. Artists use all kinds of strange materials—beer cans, old cars, peanut butter, contraceptives—to create sculptures. The advantage of these materials is that nobody can tell what the sculpture is supposed to represent, which means the work is an artistic triumph.

But the Harvard art teacher added a new dimension to this assignment. She gave each of the students in her Fundamentals of Sculpture Class a live chicken and told them to take it home and keep it around as a pet for one day.

Then they were to take it to a slaughterhouse, watch it being killed and processed, and have it for dinner.

● 252

And after picking the bones clean, they were to use them to create a work of art.

The teacher explained that her goal is to bring the artist and the object closer together.

As she said: "Because they will have eaten the chickens, the chickens will be part of their bodies. This experience will expand their imagination and understanding."

However, several of the students disagreed. They said "yucky," or words to that effect, and took their chickens to an animal shelter.

And some animal-protection groups said the project sounded disgusting.

But most of the students approved. As one Ivy League lad said, after seeing his chicken separated from its head: "It's a very interesting process. It's something you usually don't see."

That probably explains why so few Harvard grads run poultry stores.

Another student said that having the live chicken stay overnight in her dormitory was an enlightening experience. As she put it: "It's better to eat something that you had a relationship with because you respect the fact that it was alive."

I hadn't thought of relationships that way, but there is some logic in what she said. And it's a heck of a lot cheaper than going through divorce court, especially if you don't get caught.

Although I am in no position to judge the merits of the chicken-bone sculptures the students will create, I think this story illustrates why the wealthy and influential are eager to send their offspring to Harvard. It's obvious that they get educational opportunities that aren't available elsewhere.

I'm sure that if I were a Harvard parent, I'd be pleased if my kid phoned and said:

"Guess what I did for my art class today?"

"What did you do? Paint a naked lady?"

"No, I took a chicken in to have it beheaded."

It would make those hefty tuition payments seem worthwhile.

Because I want to shed my philistine and boorish attitudes, I'm going to try to learn something from this approach to the creative process.

The next time I chomp through a bucket of the Colonel's chicken and look at the stack of bones, I'll feel a sense of artistic kinsmanship with the chickens I just ate.

And when I burp, I'll tell my wife: "That ain't crude—that's art."

Endorsements
Just a Shell Game

July 16, 1985

The man from an advertising agency had an unusual proposition.

His agency does the TV commercials for a well-known chain of Mexican restaurants in Chicago.

"You may have seen our commercials," he said. "They include a cameo appearance by Lee Smith and Leon Durham of the Cubs. It shows them crunching into a tortilla."

No, I somehow missed seeing that.

"Well, anyway, we'd like to have you in a commercial."

Doing what?

"Crunching into a tortilla."

I thought tortillas were soft. I may be wrong, but I

don't think you can crunch into a tortilla. Maybe you mean a taco.

"Well, you'd be biting into some kind of Mexican food."

What else would I have to do?

"That's it. It would be a cameo appearance. You'd be seen for about four seconds. You wouldn't have to say anything."

I'd just bite into a piece of Mexican food?

"Right. For a fee, of course."

How big a fee?

He named a figure. It was not a king's ransom, but it was more than walking-around money.

"It would take about forty-five minutes to film," he said.

Amazing. In my first newspaper job almost thirty years ago, I had to work twelve weeks to earn the figure he had mentioned.

It was a small, twice-a-week paper, and I was the only police reporter, the only sports reporter, the only investigative reporter and the assistant political writer, and on Saturday I would edit the stories going into the entertainment page. The publisher believed in a day's work for an hour's pay.

Now I could make the same amount just for spending forty-five minutes biting into a taco in front of a TV camera.

And when I was in the military, it would have taken eight monthly paychecks to equal this one taco-crunching fee. Of course, I also got a bunk and meals and could attend free VD lectures.

"Well, what do you think?" he asked.

I told him I would think about it and get back to him.

So I asked Slats Grobnik, who has sound judgment, what he thought of the deal.

"That's a lot of money just to bite a taco on TV. For

255 ●

that kind of scratch, I'd bite a dog. Grab the deal."

But there is a question of ethics.

"Ethics? What's the ethics in biting a taco? Millions of people bite tacos every day. Mexicans have been biting them for hundreds of years. Are you saying that Mexicans are unethical? Careful, some of my best friends are Mexicans."

No, I'm not saying that at all. I like Mexicans, though I'm opposed to bullfighting.

"Then what's unethical?"

The truth is, I can't stand tacos.

"What has that got to do with it? I can't stand work, but I do it for the money."

It has everything to do with it. If I go on TV and bite into a taco, won't I be endorsing that taco?

"So what? You've endorsed politicians and I've never met a politician that I liked better than a taco."

But endorsing a taco I didn't like would be dishonest.

"Hey, that's the American way. Turn on your TV and look at all the people who endorse junk. Do you think they really believe what they're saying?"

Then it's wrong. Nobody should endorse a taco if they don't like a taco.

"Then tell them you'll bite something else. A tortilla or an enchilada."

But I don't like them either. The truth is, I can't stand most Mexican food. The only thing I really like is the salt on the edge of a margarita glass. Oh, and I do like tamales.

"Good, then bite a tamale."

No, because the only tamales I like are the kind that used to be sold by the little Greeks who had hot dog pushcarts on the streets. They were factory-produced tamales about the size and weight of a lead pipe. But I don't think anybody would want me to do a TV commercial for hot dog stand tamales.

"Can't you just bite the taco and spit it out when the camera is turned off?"

That would be a sham. Besides, even if I liked tacos or tortillas, what does it matter? Why should somebody eat in a restaurant because they see me biting into that restaurant's taco? Am I a taco expert? What are my credentials to tell millions of people what taco they should eat? I'm not even a Mexican.

"Well, you're a sucker to turn it down. Why, it's almost un-American. Do you think that in Russia any newsman would ever have an opportunity to make that much money by biting into a pirogi?"

That may be so. But maybe someday a food product will come along that I can lend my name to, something I can truly believe in.

"I doubt it. Not unless they start letting taverns advertise shots and beers on TV."

Robbery at 7-11?
Take a Big Gulp

July 7, 1987

There's no question that what Kays Kamalmaz did was foolish.

He was putting stock on some shelves in the 7-11 store where he works as a clerk.

A couple of guys came in, took three twelve-packs of beer from a cooler and walked out without paying for them.

Kamalmaz, twenty-six, decided he would follow them outside, jot down the license number of their car and turn it over to the police.

257

By doing that, he violated a corporate policy of his employer, the Southland Corp., which owns the huge 7-11 food store chain.

It's this company's policy that their store employees should not resist thieves or in any way interfere with them.

As a company spokesman explains it:

"We have a robbery prevention program that has various elements. They include minimizing the cash that's available in stores, improving lighting in the parking lot and around the store and the general appearance of the stores, greeting all the customers and being observant and watching the customers.

"It's designed to minimize the attractiveness or the appeal of our stores to any robbers. It's been very effective. It was suggested by an ex-convict who did time for armed robbery.

"However, should any incident of theft occur, our clerks, as part of their training, are schooled in procedures which are designed to minimize any personal injury or harm to them.

"They are told to cooperate with robbers, to do exactly as the robber says, to alert the robber to what might be any startling occurrences. For example, a fellow employee in the back who might enter the front part of the store.

"Employees are to avoid any intimidating actions and to report the incident immediately to police and management."

Although it sounds like a timid, compliant approach, it's probably a sensible policy.

After all, why should some low-pay clerk risk his life to defend a giant corporation's money?

Or, in clerk Kamalmaz's case, thirty-six cans of beer?

But Kamalmaz decided that he would play detective and get that license number.

●   258

When he walked outside, he was met by four more men who didn't want him writing down their license number and messing with their beer party.

And they gave him what would be described in Ft. Worth, which is where this occurred, as a real stompin'.

By the time they finished bashing him around the parking lot, he was a bloody mess. They broke his nose and his jaw and left him with a colorful array of welts, bruises and abrasions.

Then all six piled into their car and went off to drink their thirty-six cans of stolen beer.

The beating should have served as a lesson to Kamalmaz to follow corporate policy. Next time, smile at the thieves and maybe even say: "Have a nice day, hear?"

But the Southland Corp. decided that the beating, in itself, wasn't sufficient punishment for Kamalmaz.

After spending four days in a hospital, Kamalmaz got word that he was fired for violating corporate policy.

That seemed a bit harsh to me. So I asked the company spokesman if he couldn't have just warned Kamalmaz not to do it again. Not that a warning should have been necessary. You have to figure that a guy who got his jaw and nose broken over thirty-six cans of beer isn't likely to tackle somebody trying to run off with a can of beans or Spam.

The spokesman said: "It's such an important policy, we simply have to demonstrate it. The seriousness of the policy can't be minimized."

But all he did was go outside to get the license number. Is that against the rules?

"Absolutely. Under no circumstances do our clerks leave the store."

The spokesman said that the company regretted having to fire Kamalmaz. "But we have thousands of employees whose safety we want to promote. What this says is that the safety of our employees is foremost rather than the theft of individual items."

As I said, it's a prudent policy, and I can't disagree with it. But I still think that firing the young man was too stern. There are other ways he could have been disciplined.

I mean, if they really wanted to teach him a lesson, they could have told him that for a week he had to eat nothing but those 7-11 sandwiches.

Retired Radical
Bombs Out in Life

July 18, 1986

I hope that if he reads this, Ronald Kaufman's feelings aren't hurt. But the fact is, his name hasn't crossed my mind in almost fifteen years.

It was that long ago when Kaufman sent me a letter announcing in a self-important tone that he had planted time bombs in safe-deposit boxes in banks.

He wasn't kidding. He had indeed planted bombs in banks all over America and one of them had exploded, although it injured no one.

The letter also gave Kaufman's reasons for planting the bombs.

He fancied himself a revolutionary—part of what was known in those days as The Movement—and he wanted to change society, stir its social conscience, eliminate injustice and create some sort of utopia.

When the letter arrived, I recall being pleased. Not that I was in favor of putting bombs in banks, but it was a slow news day and it gave me something to write about.

So I wrote a column telling Kaufman that while I agreed with his goals of eliminating injustice and spreading happiness, I didn't think that putting bombs in banks was the ideal way to stir the social conscience of America, or Amerika, as he spelled it.

I tried to explain to him that most Americans were tired of rich suburban youths playing at being revolutionaries. They were tired of the Yippies chanting the F-word and the tantrum-prone Weatherman group breaking store windows. And I suggested that if he wanted to help the downtrodden, he should start at a more modest level, such as clanging a Salvation Army bell at Christmas.

That was the last I heard from Ronald Kaufman or he from me. He went "underground," as the well-born revolutionaries liked to describe it. That simply meant that in a nation of 200 million, it's easy enough to blend in, get a job, lead a normal life and duck the FBI.

And in a few days, I forgot about Kaufman. That may have hurt his feelings. He and the others in The Movement genuinely believed that their silliness was going to cause masses of Americans to rise up and follow them. They didn't understand that if any masses rose up, it would be to hang them from the nearest tree.

The reason I mention Kaufman now is that he was finally pinched the other day. After all these years, somebody recognized him and tipped off the FBI and they found him living in San Francisco and working as a janitor.

What struck me was that Kaufman, the young revolutionary, is now forty-eight years old. He's a middle-aged guy shoving a broom around an office building.

Not that there is anything demeaning about being a janitor. They're of greater value to society than most disc jockeys or politicians.

But consider Ronald's background. Because his father owned a successful business in the Milwaukee area,

Ronald could afford to get a bachelor's degree from the University of Wisconsin, then move on to Stanford and get a master's and a doctorate.

As any parent who has written tuition checks knows, it costs a small fortune to finance a kid through four years of college, much less a Ph.D.

And Ronald wasn't the kind of guy who would wait on tables or dig a ditch to get walking-around money. Not when he could be out stirring our social conscience.

So when I read about Kaufman turning up after all these years, my thoughts and sympathies immediately turned to the senior Mr. Kaufman, Ronald's father.

I don't know the man, and he might not even be around anymore, but as a tuition-paying parent myself, I had to feel for him.

After all those years of writing checks, financing all those degrees—what's he got to brag about?

A retired revolutionary who has become a middle-aged janitor.

And now Ronald is going to have to stand trial and probably spend some time—although not too much, I imagine—in a pokey.

Kids, they can break your heart.

Ronald really should have tried ringing that bell like I told him.

At Age 350, You Can Expect Senility

September 3, 1986

Harvard is celebrating its 350th year, and many newspapers and magazines are doing stories about its distinguished history and the great Americans who studied there. Young men who became presidents, senators, scholars and giants of finance, law and literature.

All of this has brought back memories of the first Harvard man I ever met.

I was about twenty-five at the time and working as editor of the midnight shift at a local news service in Chicago.

One day the boss hired a new reporter fresh out of Harvard. Although he was inexperienced, he had a quality the boss admired—a wealthy and socially prominent father.

Most of us were intrigued by having someone from that school in our midst, since the closest we had been to Harvard was when we covered a fire at 63rd and Harvard.

After a few weeks on days, tagging along with experienced reporters to learn some fundamentals, Charles was assigned to my shift to fill in for a police reporter who was on vacation.

At our first meeting, I was impressed. He wore a genuine Brooks Brothers suit with a vest. Most underpaid young reporters looked like they shopped at Goodwill outlets.

Charles turned out to be a pleasant young man, stout and prematurely balding, with a jovial manner and a tendency to refer to people as "chaps." And he assured me that he could handle any news assignment. I think he said it would be a "cup of tea."

The second night he was on my shift, midnight came but Charles didn't. At 1 A.M., he wasn't there. At 2 A.M., still no Charles.

Then the city desk phone rang and the absent Charles cheerfully said: "The most unusual thing has happened."

Yes, you're about three hours late for work.

"Right. You see, I went to my club for a late dinner."

263 ●

That in itself was unusual. Most young reporters carried late dinners in a brown bag.

"So after dinner," Charles explained, "I went into one of the reading rooms and ordered a brandy and was sitting in a chair reading a paper.

"I must have dropped off to sleep, and when I awoke the place was closed. Everything was dark. And I had to find the night watchman to let me out.

"You know, the evening manager of my club is a complete idiot for failing to notice me sleeping in that chair."

A complete idiot, I agreed.

"Well, I didn't want you too concerned. I'll be along in a while."

I thanked him for easing my worries.

A few days later, Charles was assigned to spend the night at police headquarters.

About 3 A.M., I received a phone call from a detective who asked me if Charles was one of our reporters.

When I admitted to this fact, the detective said: "We have him in custody."

For what?

"Suspicion of auto theft."

What? Charles, our Harvard man, a car thief? There must be a mistake.

I sent another reporter to police headquarters to find out what had happened.

It turned out that the detective, who specialized in auto theft, had noticed an expensive new sports car illegally parked in front of police headquarters.

The color and model jogged his memory. He checked the license plate against his current hot sheet. Sure enough, the car had been stolen the previous day.

He looked at the windshield and saw a press parking card with Charles' name on it.

He went up to the press room and asked if Charles was around.

"Pleased to meet you," said Charles, giving the detective a firm handshake.

"You're under arrest," said the cop.

Fortunately, Charles had an explanation. It was, he said, a perfectly understandable mistake.

It seemed that Charles' father rented a fleet of those sports cars for his wife, children and himself.

Charles' car had started making a pinging sound. So Charles took it to the dealer who provided the cars and told a mechanic to tune it up.

"Then," Charles said, "I took another car as a loaner."

Did you tell them that you were taking it?

"I don't think so. I assumed they'd know that I needed a replacement and took one. Can you imagine? The idiots reported it stolen."

Complete idiots, I agreed.

A few days later, Charles left my shift and, within weeks, resigned his job. On his last day, he gave me a firm handshake and said: "This has been fun, but I've decided on law school."

Harvard again? I asked.

"Yes," he said.

Good choice.

That was the last I saw of Charles. But I later heard that he had joined a respectable law firm that had many respectable clients.

So wherever he is, I offer him a distant toast on the 350th birthday of his alma mater and to all of its distinguished alumni.

And after he has the drink, I hope the manager of the club wakes Charles up.

265 ●

Phony Talk Works
on Wrong Number

February 1, 1984

Some people are angered by wrong numbers. They bellow and slam the phone down as if the caller did it on purpose.

Not me. I make the best of wrong numbers, and sometimes they can be fun.

For example, there are the little children whose parents let them play with phones.

It happens to everyone. Your phone rings and you say hello and you hear a childish voice say: "Hawwo, who dish?"

You can just hang up and be done with it. But I prefer to drop my voice to its lowest pitch, then make a loud, menacing, growling sound.

As often as not, I'll hear the phone rattle on the floor and the sound of a terrified child running away and screaming for its mommy.

I'm not being cruel. If anything, I'm helping the parents of that child lower their phone bill.

Then there was the man who dialed my home number one night and, when my son answered the phone, mumbled: "Lemme talk to Delia."

My son politely said: "What number do you want?"

The man mumbled an obscenity and hung up.

A minute later, the phone rang again. I picked it up. It was the same guy. He mumbled: "Lemme talk to Delia."

Now, had he been polite the first time, I would have told him that he was dialing the wrong number. Instead, I snarled:

"What do you want with Delia, bub?"

● 266

That woke him up, and he yelled: "Who the hell are you?"

Actually, his language was much stronger. So I said: "Never mind that. Who are you?"

He said: "Hey, I'm Delia's boyfriend."

I said: "Hold on." Then I yelled, so he could hear me: "Hey, Delia, there's some klutz on the phone who says he's your boyfriend."

I waited a moment, then said: "Delia says she don't want to talk to any klutz."

He began shouting and swearing both at me and Delia. So I interrupted and said: "Take my advice, pal. Delia is too good for a no-good, low-life bum like you, so you better straighten out your act or you're going to be aced out."

Then I hung up. He never called back, so I assume he accepted my counseling and now he and Delia probably have a much more stable relationship.

Which brings me to my most recent wrong number.

This morning my office phone rang, and when I answered, a woman began speaking in a crisp, businesslike manner.

She said she was with a Los Angeles firm that does corporate research and wanted to ask me some questions about corporate policies at this company.

"Are you the comptroller at your corporation?" she asked.

"No."

"Oh, I asked your switchboard for the comptroller's office."

"Maybe he's not around."

"I see. Well, could you answer my questions?"

"Sure, why not. As long as they don't have to do with corporate secrets."

"No, I don't think they will."

"Okay."

"All right. Now, how many employees does your company have?"

"Oh, we've got.lots of them."

"Lots?"

"Sure, lots and lots. We've got them all over the place. You should see it."

"Could you be more specific in terms of numbers of employees?"

"Well, that's hard to do. We really don't count them because they're always moving around. It's hard to make a headcount. But we've got thousands and thousands of them, I can tell you that."

"Are there more than 5,000?"

"Are you kidding? We've probably got ten times that many. I mean, this is no ma and pa grocery store, you know."

"I see. Well, can I ask you about your policy on corporate credit cards?"

"No credit cards. No sirree."

"Why is that?"

"Listen, you start giving people credit cards, and how do you know what they're going to buy with them. First thing you know, they're buying expensive gifts for their girlfriends. Perfume. Jewelry. Eating in French restaurants. Some people are weak."

"Well, do your employees travel?"

"Some do, some don't. Depends on if they're going somewhere."

"How do you handle payment for travel without credit cards?"

"We give them a few bucks cash, and tell them: 'When that runs out, get your ass back here.' "

"I see. Well, that's an interesting policy."

"I think so."

● 268

"Could I have your name please?"

I gave her my name.

"And what is your title?"

"Uh, we don't go in for all those traditional corporate titles."

"Well, are you the chief executive officer?"

"I really don't like to use that title."

"What title do you use?"

"Well, they call me the Big Heat."

"The Big Heat?"

"Yep. Got it on my office door. Looks real good."

"The Big Heat."

"Yeah. Or just plain Heat for short."

"Well, I've never heard of corporate titles like those before."

"I guess the trend hasn't reached California yet."

"I guess not. Well, thank you. Good-bye."

"By-dee-by."

When she submits her report, I'm sure it will create a stir at her firm.

And I wouldn't be surprised if we soon start reading stories in the financial pages about corporate boards in California naming some executive to the post of Big Heat.

When that happens, remember where it started.

Criminal's Death
Was a Crime

October 8, 1985

It's a widely held belief that our society's legal system coddles criminals. But that's not always so. Society can be pretty tough on some wrongdoers.

Just consider the case of Kathryn Ann Entress, who recently got in trouble with the law.

At first glance, you wouldn't think that Miss Entress, thirty-seven, was capable of committing a crime. Or at second and third glance.

Only five feet tall and barely weighing a hundred pounds, she seemed more frail than a bird.

And her tiny body was often racked by terrible fits of asthmatic gasping, wheezing and coughing.

But looks can be deceiving. It appears that beneath this pathetic exterior was a criminal. A thief, to be precise.

She wasn't always a criminal. At one time she was a postal worker. But her chronic breathing problems kept her from working regularly, so she was given a small disability pension.

That's when she wound up living in a drab trailer park outside Ft. Lauderdale, Florida. Just her and her cat, whose name is unknown, in the sparsely furnished trailer.

There are a lot of people like her in Florida. The vegetation and many of the residents don't have deep roots.

It was in the trailer park that Miss Entress turned to crime and got in trouble with the law.

In fairness, she wasn't trying to get rich fast, as some criminals do.

Her motive was thirst. And a desire for personal hygiene.

Because she was of modest means, to say the least, Miss Entress sometimes had trouble making ends meet. She didn't live high, but by the time she paid her rent, bought the groceries and a few scraps for her cat, she didn't have much spendable income.

So sometimes she couldn't cover all the bills. And one bill she fell behind on was water. When she fell far enough behind, her water was cut off.

Water is something most of us take for granted. Like air. But when you don't have enough of either of them, life can be hard.

And that was what happened to Miss Entress. When her water was cut off, she began taking jugs to the trailer park's laundry room, filling them and carrying them back to her trailer.

Because of her asthma, her air would sometimes be cut off. So she would have to stop, put the jugs down and use an inhaler to get her breathing again.

She finally couldn't take it any more, all that hauling of the heavy water jugs, especially in Florida's summer heat. So she found a way to turn the water on in her trailer.

And that made her a criminal. She was stealing water, because she wasn't paying for it.

Eventually her crime was detected. The investigation was made, the papers were filled out and the cops came to get her.

Her bond was set at $250. That's not a fortune, but to somebody who has to steal water, it's more than walking-around money.

She couldn't make bond, so she was taken to the Broward County Jail and put alone in a cell in the women's section.

I'm not sure what the penalty is for stealing water in Broward County, Florida. But I do know what Miss Entress' punishment was.

When she was jailed, her inhaler was taken away from her. It's the policy in most jails that inmates be stripped of all personal possessions.

And though an inhaler is a harmless enough device—you can buy them in any drugstore—the rules are the rules are the rules.

So sometime during her second night in jail, Miss

271 ●

Entress had an asthma attack. Nobody heard her wheezing, coughing and gasping for breath.

When somebody finally looked in her cell, she was dead.

The coroner's physician, who examined her body, said that if she'd had an inhaler, she probably would be alive.

So don't tell me we're easy on criminals. Maybe some of them. But even the most skeptical law-and-order zealots will have to admit that death by choking is a pretty severe penalty for filching some water.

I don't know what happened to her cat.

Windshield-Wiper
Lets in Some Light

August 21, 1987

There are some mornings so lousy that you know the rest of the day is going to stink.

This one began with nature as the enemy in the form of a flooded basement. Nature is a frustrating enemy because no matter how much you rant and swear, it doesn't listen.

Then came the writing of a large check to the Internal Revenue Service. The IRS is a dangerous enemy because if you rant and swear you might be audited and have even more to rant and swear about.

And before the morning was half over, there was technology, an old and hated foe. It took the form of the Ohio Street bridge going up, then getting stuck and not coming down for thirty minutes, trapping thousands of us in our cars with nowhere to go.

There's not much point in cursing a Chicago bridge-tender. If anything, we should have been grateful that he was sober enough not to raise the bridge while any of us were on it.

By the time the bridge lowered, and the traffic crept forward, I was hopelessly late for an interview with a source, my teeth were grinding and I was sure the entire world was plotting against me.

At Clark Street, I just caught the red light. That got me even angrier.

Suddenly, water was being sloshed across my windshield. At first, I didn't know where it was coming from.

Then I saw that a teenager had stepped from the curb with one of those gas-station tools, a combination sponge and squeegee, for cleaning windshields.

And he got me mad, too. My windshield was already spotless, so why was he cleaning it? Who asked him to? The light might change and I could lose a few more precious seconds.

Before he could use the squeegee, I gave him an angry glare, waved him off and turned on my wipers.

He stepped back on the sidewalk, shrugged, shook his head slightly and turned away.

About sixteen and very skinny. His T-shirt was a grimy gray and his trousers looked like the kind that might have sold for $8 new a long time ago.

The light turned green, and I drove ahead. By the time I got to the next corner, I realized what I had just done.

That wasn't one of my sons on a corner, washing the windshields of strangers' cars, hoping some of them would be generous enough to hand him two bits. My sons never had to do anything that demeaning to put a few dollars in their pockets. They were fortunate enough to have been born Caucasian Americans, with an overpaid father.

And there I sat, in my big, black, fat-cat car, with air-conditioning blasting, stereo playing and enough electronic doodads to do everything but blow my nose.

I had enough money in my pocket to buy that skinny kid a suit, pay his family's rent for a month and maybe fill up their refrigerator and pantry.

But I hadn't had the decency to let him squeegee the windshield, then touch the button that lowers a window and give him a buck and a smile. I had given him a scowl and a wave-off, gestures that said he was a nothing.

And all the while, do you know what was playing on my stereo cassette? Peter, Paul and Mary singing that if they had a hammer, they'd hammer out love between their brothers and their sisters, all over the world—that's what was playing.

While I'm telling some ghetto kid to get lost.

Statistics ran through my mind. What's the teen-age black unemployment rate—40 or 50 percent? And we wonder why so many are into crime?

But there was a kid who wasn't grabbing my hubcaps, smashing and grabbing, mugging or heisting. All he was doing was cleaning windshields and hoping people like me might appreciate it.

Sure, it was a form of panhandling. But with that sponge and squeegee, he gave dignity to it. He was saying: "Look, I'm trying to work. I'm doing *something.*"

And I tell him to bug off.

So I made a right turn at the next corner, then another one. I figured I'd double back and catch him a second time, and this time I'd give him a five-spot.

By the time I got back to the corner, he was gone. Maybe he moved to another corner. So I went around again, tried a couple more streets. But I couldn't find him.

So I drove to the office and parked. When I walked past my assistant, she said, "Good morning."

● 274

I told her it was a lousy, stinking morning.

Then I went in the men's room, looked in the mirror and saw the biggest reason for it being a lousy, stinking morning.